MY REMINISCENCES

MY REMINISCENCES

BY

SIR RABINDRANATH TAGORE

GYAN

Published by

Gyan Publishing House
5, Ansari Road
Daryaganj, New Delhi-110002
Phone: 011-47034999, 9811692060
E-mail: books@gyanbooks.com

Distribution Network
gyanbooks.com
India, USA, Canada, UK, Australia

ISBN: 978-81-212-8452-3 (HB)
First Published, 1912

2nd Impression 2024

Printed at: Gyan Press, Delhi.

MY REMINISCENCES
Author: RABINDRANATH TAGORE

MY REMINISCENCES

RABINDRANATH TAGORE

FROM THE PORTRAIT IN COLORS BY SASI KUMAR HESH

MY REMINISCENCES

BY

SIR RABINDRANATH TAGORE

WITH FRONTISPIECE FROM THE PORTRAIT
IN COLORS BY SASI KUMAR HESH

New York
THE MACMILLAN COMPANY
1917

Set up and electrotyped. Published April, 1917.

TRANSLATOR'S PREFACE

THESE Reminiscences were written and published by the Author in his fiftieth year, shortly before he started on a trip to Europe and America for his failing health in 1912. It was in the course of this trip that he wrote for the first time in the English language for publication.

In these memory pictures, so lightly, even casually presented by the author there is, nevertheless, revealed a connected history of his inner life together with that of the varying literary forms in which his growing self found successive expression, up to the point at which both his soul and poetry attained maturity.

This lightness of manner and importance of matter form a combination the translation of which into a different language is naturally a matter of considerable difficulty. It was, in any case, a task which the present Translator, not being an original writer in the English language, would hardly have ventured to undertake, had there not been other considerations. The translator's familiarity, however, with the persons, scenes, and events herein depicted made it a temptation difficult for him to resist, as well as a responsibility which he did not care to leave to others not possessing these advantages, and therefore more liable to miss a point, or give a wrong impression.

The Translator, moreover, had the author's permission and advice to make a free translation, a portion of which was completed and approved by the latter before he left India on his recent tour to Japan and America.

In regard to the nature of the freedom taken for the purposes of the translation, it may be mentioned that those suggestions which might not have been as clear to the foreign as to the Bengali reader have been brought out in a slightly more elaborate manner than in the original text; while again, in rare cases, others which depend on allusions entirely unfamiliar to the non-Indian reader, have been omitted rather than spoil by an over-elaboration the simplicity and naturalness which is the great feature of the original.

There are no footnotes in the original. All the footnotes here given have been added by the Translator in the hope that they may be of further assistance to the foreign reader.

CONTENTS

LIST OF ILLUSTRATIONS

PART I

MY REMINISCENCES

(1)

I KNOW not who paints the pictures on memory's canvas; but whoever he may be, what he is painting are pictures; by which I mean that he is not there with his brush simply to make a faithful copy of all that is happening. He takes in and leaves out according to his taste. He makes many a big thing small and small thing big. He has no compunction in putting into the background that which was to the fore, or bringing to the front that which was behind. In short he is painting pictures, and not writing history.

Thus, over Life's outward aspect passes the series of events, and within is being painted a set of pictures. The two correspond but are not one.

We do not get the leisure to view thoroughly this studio within us. Portions of it now and then catch our eye, but the greater part remains out of sight in the darkness. Why the ever-busy painter is painting; when he will have done; for what gallery his pictures are destined—who can tell?

Some years ago, on being questioned as to the events of my past life, I had occasion to pry into this picture-chamber. I had thought to be content with selecting some few materials for my Life's story. I then discovered, as I opened the door, that Life's memories are not Life's history, but the original work of an unseen Artist. The variegated colours scattered about are not reflections of outside lights, but belong to the painter himself, and come passion-tinged from his heart; thereby unfitting the record on the canvas for use as evidence in a court of law.

But though the attempt to gather precise history from memory's storehouse may be fruitless, there is a fascination in looking over the pictures, a fascination which cast its spell on me.

The road over which we journey, the wayside shelter in which we pause, are not pictures while yet we travel—they are too necessary, too obvious. When, however, before turning into the evening resthouse, we look back upon the cities, fields, rivers and hills which we have been through in Life's morning, then, in the light of the passing day, are they pictures indeed. Thus, when my opportunity came, did I look back, and was engrossed.

Was this interest aroused within me solely by

a natural affection for my own past? Some personal feeling, of course, there must have been, but the pictures had also an independent artistic value of their own. There is no event in my reminiscences worthy of being preserved for all time. But the quality of the subject is not the only justification for a record. What one has truly felt, if only it can be made sensible to others, is always of importance to one's fellow men. If pictures which have taken shape in memory can be brought out in words, they are worth a place in literature.

It is as literary material that I offer my memory pictures. To take them as an attempt at autobiography would be a mistake. In such a view these reminiscences would appear useless as well as incomplete.

(2) *Teaching Begins*

We three boys were being brought up together. Both my companions were two years older than I. When they were placed under their tutor, my teaching also began, but of what I learnt nothing remains in my memory.

What constantly recurs to me is "The rain patters, the leaf quivers."[1] I am just come to

[1] A jingling sentence in the Bengali Child's Primer.

anchor after crossing the stormy region of the *kara, khala* [1] series; and I am reading "The rain patters, the leaf quivers," for me the first poem of the Arch Poet. Whenever the joy of that day comes back to me, even now, I realise why rhyme is so needful in poetry. Because of it the words come to an end, and yet end not; the utterance is over, but not its ring; and the ear and the mind can go on and on with their game of tossing the rhyme to each other. Thus did the rain patter and the leaves quiver again and again, the live-long day in my consciousness.

Another episode of this period of my early boyhood is held fast in my mind.

We had an old cashier, Kailash by name, who was like one of the family. He was a great wit, and would be constantly cracking jokes with everybody, old and young; recently married sons-in-law, new comers into the family circle, being his special butts. There was room for the suspicion that his humour had not deserted him even after death. Once my elders were engaged in an attempt to start a postal service with the other world by means of a planchette. At one of the sittings the pencil scrawled out the name of Kailash. He was asked as to the sort of life one led where he was. Not a bit of it, was the

[1] Exercises in two-syllables.

reply. "Why should you get so cheap what I had to die to learn?"

This Kailash used to rattle off for my special delectation a doggerel ballad of his own composition. The hero was myself and there was a glowing anticipation of the arrival of a heroine. And as I listened my interest would wax intense at the picture of this world-charming bride illuminating the lap of the future in which she sat enthroned. The list of the jewellery with which she was bedecked from head to foot, and the unheard of splendour of the preparations for the bridal, might have turned older and wiser heads; but what moved the boy, and set wonderful joy pictures flitting before his vision, was the rapid jingle of the frequent rhymes and the swing of the rhythm.

These two literary delights still linger in my memory—and there is the other, the infants' classic: "The rain falls pit-a-pat, the tide comes up the river."

The next thing I remember is the beginning of my school-life. One day I saw my elder brother, and my sister's son Satya, also a little older than myself, starting off to school, leaving me behind, accounted unfit. I had never before ridden in a carriage nor even been out of the house. So when Satya came back, full of unduly glowing accounts of his adventures on the way, I felt I simply could not stay at home. Our tutor tried to dispel my illusion with sound advice and a resounding slap: "You're crying to go to school now, you'll have to cry a lot more to be let off later on." I have no recollection of the name, features or disposition of this tutor of ours, but the impression of his weighty advice and weightier hand has not yet faded. Never in my life have I heard a truer prophecy.

My crying drove me prematurely into the Oriental Seminary. What I learnt there I have no idea, but one of its methods of punishment I still bear in mind. The boy who was unable to repeat his lessons was made to stand on a bench with arms extended, and on his upturned palms were piled a number of slates. It is for psychologists to debate how far this method is likely to conduce to a better grasp of things. I thus began my schooling at an extremely tender age.

My initiation into literature had its origin, at the same time, in the books which were in vogue in the servants' quarters. Chief among these were a Bengali translation of Chanakya's aphorisms, and the Ramayana of Krittivasa.

A picture of one day's reading of the Ramayana comes clearly back to me.

The day was a cloudy one. I was playing

Rabindranath Tagore in 1877

about in the long verandah[1] overlooking the road. All of a sudden Satya, for some reason I do not remember, wanted to frighten me by shouting, "Policeman! Policeman!" My ideas of the duties of policemen were of an extremely vague description. One thing I was certain about, that a person charged with crime once placed in a policeman's hands would, as sure as the wretch caught in a crocodile's serrated grip, go under and be seen no more. Not knowing how an innocent boy could escape this relentless penal code, I bolted towards the inner apartments, with shudders running down my back for blind fear of pursuing policemen. I broke to my mother the news of my impending doom, but it did not seem to disturb her much. However, not deeming it safe to venture out again, I sat down on the sill of my mother's door to read the dog-eared Ramayana, with a marbled paper cover, which belonged to her old aunt. Alongside stretched the verandah running round the four sides of the open inner quadrangle, on which had fallen the faint afternoon glow of the clouded sky, and finding me

[1] Roofed colonnade or balcony. The writer's family house is an irregular three-storied mass of buildings, which had grown with the joint family it sheltered, built round several courtyards or quadrangles, with long colonnades along the outer faces, and narrower galleries running round each quadrangle, giving access to the single rows of rooms.

weeping over one of its sorrowful situations my great-aunt came and took away the book from me.

(3) *Within and Without*

Luxury was a thing almost unknown in the days of my infancy. The standard of living was then, as a whole, much more simple than it is now. Apart from that, the children of our household were entirely free from the fuss of being too much looked after. The fact is that, while the process of looking after may be an occasional treat for the guardians, to the children it is always an unmitigated nuisance.

We used to be under the rule of the servants. To save themselves trouble they had almost suppressed our right of free movement. But the freedom of not being petted made up even for the harshness of this bondage, for our minds were left clear of the toils of constant coddling, pampering and dressing-up.

Our food had nothing to do with delicacies. A list of our articles of clothing would only invite the modern boy's scorn. On no pretext did we wear socks or shoes till we had passed our tenth year. In the cold weather a second cotton tunic over the first one sufficed. It never entered our heads to consider ourselves ill-off for that reason.

It was only when old Niyamat, the tailor, would forget to put a pocket into one of our tunics that we complained, for no boy has yet been born so poor as not to have the wherewithal to stuff his pockets; nor, by a merciful dispensation of providence, is there much difference between the wealth of boys of rich and of poor parentage. We used to have a pair of slippers each, but not always where we had our feet. Our habit of kicking the slippers on ahead, and catching them up again, made them work none the less hard, through effectually defeating at every step the reason of their being.

Our elders were in every way at a great distance from us, in their dress and food, living and doing, conversation and amusement. We caught glimpses of these, but they were beyond our reach. Elders have become cheap to modern children; they are too readily accessible, and so are all objects of desire. Nothing ever came so easily to us. Many a trivial thing was for us a rarity, and we lived mostly in the hope of attaining, when we were old enough, the things which the distant future held in trust for us. The result was that what little we did get we enjoyed to the utmost; from skin to core nothing was thrown away. The modern child of a well-to-do family nibbles at only half the things he gets; the greater part of his world is wasted on him.

Our days were spent in the servants' quarters in the south-east corner of the outer apartments. One of our servants was Shyam, a dark chubby boy with curly locks, hailing from the District of Khulna. He would put me into a selected spot and, tracing a chalk line all round, warn me with solemn face and uplifted finger of the perils of transgressing this ring. Whether the threatened danger was material or spiritual I never fully understood, but a great fear used to possess me. I had read in the Ramayana of the tribulations of Sita for having left the ring drawn by Lakshman, so it was not possible for me to be sceptical of its potency.

Just below the window of this room was a tank with a flight of masonry steps leading down into the water; on its west bank, along the garden wall, an immense banyan tree; to the south a fringe of cocoanut palms. Ringed round as I was near this window I would spend the whole day peering through the drawn venetian shutters, gazing and gazing on this scene as on a picture book. From early morning our neighbours would drop in one by one to have their bath. I knew the time for each one to arrive. I was familiar with the peculiarities of each one's toilet. One would stop up his ears with his fingers as he took his regulation number of dips, after which he would depart. Another would not venture on a complete immersion but be content with only squeezing his wet towel repeatedly over his head. A third would carefully drive the surface impurities away from him with a rapid play of his arms, and then on a sudden impulse take his plunge. There was one who jumped in from the top steps without any preliminaries at all. Another would walk slowly in, step by step, muttering his morning prayers the while. One was always in a hurry, hastening home as soon as he was through with his dip. Another was in no sort of hurry at all, taking his bath leisurely, followed with a good rub-down, and a change from wet bathing clothes into clean ones, including a careful adjustment of the folds of his waist cloth, ending with a turn or two in the outer [1] garden, and the gathering of flowers, with which he would finally saunter slowly homewards, radiating the cool comfort of his refreshed body, as he went. This would go on till it was past noon. Then the bathing places would be deserted and become silent. Only the ducks remained, paddling about after water snails, or busy preening their feathers, the live-long day.

When solitude thus reigned over the water, my whole attention would be drawn to the shad-

[1] The men's portion of the house is the outer; and the women's the inner.

ows under the banyan tree. Some of its aerial roots, creeping down along its trunk, had formed a dark complication of coils at its base. It seemed as if into this mysterious region the laws of the universe had not found entrance; as if some old-world dream-land had escaped the divine vigilance and lingered on into the light of modern day. Whom I used to see there, and what those beings did, it is not possible to express in intelligible language. It was about this banyan tree that I wrote later:

With tangled roots hanging down from your branches,
O ancient banyan tree,
You stand still day and night, like an ascetic at his
penances,
Do you ever remember the child whose fancy played
with your shadows?

Alas! that banyan tree is no more, nor the piece of water which served to mirror the majestic forest-lord! Many of those who used to bathe there have also followed into oblivion the shade of the banyan tree. And that boy, grown older, is counting the alternations of light and darkness which penetrate the complexities with which the roots he has thrown off on all sides have encircled him.

Going out of the house was forbidden to us, in fact we had not even the freedom of all its parts. We perforce took our peeps at nature from behind the barriers. Beyond my reach there was this limitless thing called the Outside, of which flashes and sounds and scents used momentarily to come and touch me through its interstices. It seemed to want to play with me through the bars with so many gestures. But it was free and I was bound—there was no way of meeting. So the attraction was all the stronger. The chalk line has been wiped away to-day, but the confining ring is still there. The distant is just as distant, the outside is still beyond me; and I am reminded of the poem I wrote when I was older:

The tame bird was in a cage, the free bird was in the forest,
They met when the time came, it was a decree of fate.
The free bird cries, "O my love, let us fly to wood."
The cage bird whispers, "Come hither, let us both live in the cage."
Says the free bird, "Among bars, where is there room to spread one's wings?"
"Alas," cries the cage bird, "I should not know where to sit perched in the sky."

The parapets of our terraced roofs were higher than my head. When I had grown taller; when the tyranny of the servants had relaxed; when, with the coming of a newly married bride into the house, I had achieved some recognition as a companion of her leisure, then did I sometimes come up to the terrace in the middle of the day. By that time everybody in the house would have finished their meal; there would be an interval in the business of the household; over the inner apartments would rest the quiet of the midday siesta; the wet bathing clothes would be hanging over the parapets to dry; the crows would be picking at the leavings thrown on the refuse heap at the corner of the yard; in the solitude of that interval the caged bird would, through the gaps in the parapet, commune bill to bill with the free bird!

I would stand and gaze. . . . My glance first falls on the row of cocoanut trees on the further edge of our inner garden. Through these are seen the "Singhi's Garden" with its cluster of huts [1] and tank, and on the edge of the tank the dairy of our milkwoman, Tara; still further on, mixed up with the tree-tops, the various shapes and different heights of the terraced roofs of Calcutta, flashing back the blazing whiteness of the midday sun, stretch right away into the grayish blue of the eastern horizon. And some of these far distant

[1] These Bustees or settlements consisting of tumbledown hovels, existing side by side with palatial buildings, are still one of the anomalies of Calcutta. *Tr.*

The Inner Garden was My Paradise

dwellings from which stand forth their roofed stairways leading up to the terrace, look as if with uplifted finger and a wink they are hinting to me of the mysteries of their interiors. Like the beggar at the palace door who imagines impossible treasures to be held in the strong rooms closed to him, I can hardly tell of the wealth of play and freedom which these unknown dwellings seem to me crowded with. From the furthest depth of the sky full of burning sunshine overhead the thin shrill cry of a kite reaches my ear; and from the lane adjoining Singhi's Garden comes up, past the houses silent in their noonday slumber, the sing-song of the bangle-seller—*chai choori chai* . . . and my whole being would fly away from the work-a-day world.

My father hardly ever stayed at home, he was constantly roaming about. His rooms on the third storey used to remain shut up. I would pass my hands through the venetian shutters, and thus opening the latch get the door open, and spend the afternoon lying motionless on his sofa at the south end. First of all it was a room always closed, and then there was the stolen entry, this gave it a deep flavour of mystery; further the broad empty expanse of terrace to the south, glowing in the rays of the sun would set me day-dreaming.

There was yet another attraction. The waterworks had just been started in Calcutta, and in the first exuberance of its triumphant entry it did not stint even the Indian quarters of their supply. In that golden age of pipe water, it used to flow even up to my father's third storey rooms. And turning on the shower tap I would indulge to my heart's content in an untimely bath. Not so much for the comfort of it, as to give rein to my desire to do just as I fancied. The alternation of the joy of liberty, and the fear of being caught, made that shower of municipal water send arrows of delight thrilling into me.

It was perhaps because the possibility of contact with the outside was so remote that the joy of it came to me so much more readily. When material is in profusion, the mind gets lazy and leaves everything to it, forgetting that for a successful feast of joy its internal equipment counts for more than the external. This is the chief lesson which his infant state has to teach to man. There his possessions are few and trivial, yet he needs no more for his happiness. The world of play is spoilt for the unfortunate youngster who is burdened with an unlimited quantity of playthings.

To call our inner garden a garden is to say a deal too much. Its properties consisted of a citron tree, a couple of plum trees of different varieties, and a row of cocoanut trees. In the centre was a paved circle the cracks of which various grasses and weeds had invaded and planted in them their victorious standards. Only those flowering plants which refused to die of neglect continued uncomplainingly to perform their respective duties without casting any aspersions on the gardener. In the northern corner was a rice-husking shed, where the inmates of the inner apartments would occasionally foregather when household necessity demanded. This last vestige of rural life has since owned defeat and slunk away ashamed and unnoticed.

None the less I suspect that Adam's garden of Eden could hardly have been better adorned than this one of ours; for he and his paradise were alike naked; they needed not to be furnished with material things. It is only since his tasting of the fruit of the tree of knowledge, and till he can fully digest it, that man's need for external furniture and embellishment persistently grows. Our inner garden was my paradise; it was enough for me. I well remember how in the early autumn dawn I would run there as soon as I was awake. A scent of dewy grass and foliage would rush to meet me, and the morning with its cool fresh sunlight would peep out at me over the top of the Eastern garden wall from below the trembling tassels of the cocoanut palms.

There is another piece of vacant land to the north of the house which to this day we call the *golabari* (barn house). The name shows that in some remote past this must have been the place where the year's store of grain used to be kept in a barn. Then, as with brother and sister in infancy, the likeness between town and country was visible all over. Now the family resemblance can hardly be traced. This *golabari* would be my holiday haunt if I got the chance. It would hardly be correct to say that I went there to play—it was the place not play, which drew me. Why this was so, is difficult to tell. Perhaps its being a deserted bit of waste land lying in an out-of-the-way corner gave it its charm for me. It was entirely outside the living quarters and bore no stamp of usefulness; moreover it was as unadorned as it was useless, for no one had ever planted anything there; it was doubtless for these reasons that this desert spot offered no resistance to the free play of the boy's imagination. Whenever I got any loop-hole to evade the vigilance of my warders and could contrive to reach the *golabari*, I felt I had a holiday indeed.

There was yet another place in our house which I have even yet not succeeded in finding out.

A little girl playmate of my own age called this the "King's palace."[1] "I have just been there," she would sometimes tell me. But somehow the propitious moment never turned up when she could take me along with her. That was a wonderful place, and its playthings were as wonderful as the games that were played there. It seemed to me it must be somewhere very near—perhaps in the first or second storey; the only thing was one never seemed to be able to get there. How often have I asked my companion, "Only tell me, is it really inside the house or outside?" And she would always reply, "No, no, it's in this very house." I would sit and wonder: "Where then can it be? Don't I know all the rooms of the house?" Who the king might be I never cared to inquire; where his palace is still remains undiscovered; this much was clear—the king's palace was within our house.

Looking back on childhood's days the thing that recurs most often is the mystery which used to fill both life and world. Something undreamt of was lurking everywhere and the uppermost question every day was: when, Oh! when would we come across it? It was as if nature held something in her closed hands and was smilingly asking us: "What d'you think I have?" What was

[1] Corresponding to "Wonderland."

impossible for her to have was the thing we had no idea of.

Well do I remember the custard apple seed which I had planted and kept in a corner of the south verandah, and used to water every day. The thought that the seed might possibly grow into a tree kept me in a great state of fluttering wonder. Custard apple seeds still have the habit of sprouting, but no longer to the accompaniment of that feeling of wonder. The fault is not in the custard apple but in the mind. We had once stolen some rocks from an elder cousin's rockery and started a little rockery of our own. The plants which we sowed in its interstices were cared for so excessively that it was only because of their vegetable nature that they managed to put up with it till their untimely death. Words cannot recount the endless joy and wonder which this miniature mountain-top held for us. We had no doubt that this creation of ours would be a wonderful thing to our elders also. The day that we sought to put this to the proof, however, the hillock in the corner of our room, with all its rocks, and all its vegetation, vanished. The knowledge that the schoolroom floor was not a proper foundation for the erection of a mountain was imparted so rudely, and with such suddenness, that it gave us a considerable shock. The weight of stone of which the floor was relieved settled on our minds when we realised the gulf between our fancies and the will of our elders.

How intimately did the life of the world throb for us in those days! Earth, water, foliage and sky, they all spoke to us and would not be disregarded. How often were we struck by the poignant regret that we could only see the upper storey of the earth and knew nothing of its inner storey. All our planning was as to how we could pry beneath its dust-coloured cover. If, thought we, we could drive in bamboo after bamboo, one over the other, we might perhaps get into some sort of touch with its inmost depths.

During the *Magh* festival a series of wooden pillars used to be planted round the outer courtyard for supporting the chandeliers. Digging holes for these would begin on the first of *Magh*. The preparations for festivity are ever interesting to young folk. But this digging had a special attraction for me. Though I had watched it done year after year—and seen the hole grow bigger and bigger till the digger had completely disappeared inside, and yet nothing extraordinary, nothing worthy of the quest of prince or knight, had ever appeared—yet every time I had the feeling that the lid being lifted off a chest of mystery. I felt that a little bit more digging would do it.

Year after year passed, but that bit never got done. There was a pull at the curtain but it was not drawn. The elders, thought I, can do whatever they please, why do they rest content with such shallow delving? If we young folk had the ordering of it, the inmost mystery of the earth would no longer be allowed to remain smothered in its dust covering.

And the thought that behind every part of the vault of blue reposed the mysteries of the sky would also spur our imaginings. When our Pundit, in illustration of some lesson in our Bengali science primer, told us that the blue sphere was not an enclosure, how thunderstruck we were! "Put ladder upon ladder," said he, "and go on mounting away, but you will never bump your head." He must be sparing of his ladders, I opined, and questioned with a rising inflection, "And what if we put more ladders, and more, and more?" When I realised that it was fruitless multiplying ladders I remained dumbfounded pondering over the matter. Surely, I concluded, such an astounding piece of news must be known only to those who are the world's schoolmasters!

PART II

(4) *Servocracy*

IN the history of India the regime of the Slave Dynasty was not a happy one. In going back to the reign of the servants in my own life's history I can find nothing glorious or cheerful touching the period. There were frequent changes of king, but never a variation in the code of restraints and punishments with which we were afflicted. We, however, had no opportunity at the time for philosophising on the subject; our backs bore as best they could the blows which befell them: and we accepted as one of the laws of the universe that it is for the Big to hurt and for the Small to be hurt. It has taken me a long time to learn the opposite truth that it is the Big who suffer and the Small who cause suffering.

The quarry does not view virtue and vice from the standpoint of the hunter. That is why the alert bird, whose cry warns its fellows before the shot has sped, gets abused as vicious. We howled when we were beaten, which our chastisers did not consider good manners; it was in fact counted sedition against the servocracy. I cannot forget how, in order effectively to suppress such sedition, our heads used to be crammed into the huge water jars then in use; distasteful, doubtless, was this outcry to those who caused it; moreover, it was likely to have unpleasant consequences.

I now sometimes wonder why such cruel treatment was meted out to us by the servants. I cannot admit that there was on the whole anything in our behaviour or demeanour to have put us beyond the pale of human kindness. The real reason must have been that the whole of our burden was thrown on the servants, and the whole burden is a thing difficult to bear even for those who are nearest and dearest. If children are only allowed to be children, to run and play about and satisfy their curiosity, it becomes quite simple. Insoluble problems are only created if you try to confine them inside, keep them still or hamper their play. Then does the burden of the child, so lightly borne by its own childishness, fall heavily on the guardian—like that of the horse in the fable which was carried instead of being allowed to trot on its own legs: and though money procured bearers even for such a burden it could not prevent them taking it out of the unlucky beast at every step.

Of most of these tyrants of our childhood I remember only their cuffings and boxings, and nothing more. Only one personality stands out in my memory.

His name was Iswar. He had been a village schoolmaster before. He was a prim, proper and sedately dignified personage. The Earth seemed too earthy for him, with too little water to keep it sufficiently clean; so that he had to be in a constant state of warfare with its chronic soiled state. He would shoot his water-pot into the tank with a lightning movement so as to get his supply from an uncontaminated depth. It was he who, when bathing in the tank, would be continually thrusting away the surface impurities till he took a sudden plunge expecting, as it were, to catch the water unawares. When walking his right arm stood out at an angle from his body, as if, so it seemed to us, he could not trust the cleanliness even of his own garments. His whole bearing had the appearance of an effort to keep clear of the imperfections which, through unguarded avenues, find entrance into earth, water and air, and into the ways of men. Unfathomable was the depth of his gravity. With head slightly tilted he would mince his carefully selected words in a deep voice. His literary diction would give food for merriment to our elders behind his back, some of his high-flown phrases finding a permanent place in our family repertoire of witticisms. But I doubt whether the expressions he used would sound as remarkable to-day; showing how the literary and spoken languages, which used to be as sky from earth asunder, are now coming nearer each other.

This erstwhile schoolmaster had discovered a way of keeping us quiet in the evenings. Every evening he would gather us round the cracked castor-oil lamp and read out to us stories from the Ramayana and Mahabharata. Some of the other servants would also come and join the audience. The lamp would be throwing huge shadows right up to the beams of the roof, the little house lizards catching insects on the walls, the bats doing a mad dervish dance round and round the verandahs outside, and we listening in silent open-mouthed wonder.

I still remember, on the evening we came to the story of Kusha and Lava, and those two valiant lads were threatening to humble to the dust the renown of their father and uncles, how the tense silence of that dimly lighted room was bursting with eager anticipation. It was getting late, our prescribed period of wakefulness was drawing to a close, and yet the dénouement was far off.

At this critical juncture my father's old follower Kishori came to the rescue, and finished the episode for us, at express speed, to the quickstep of Dasuraya's jingling verses. The impression of the soft slow chant of Krittivasa's [1] fourteen-syllabled measure was swept clean away and we were left

[1] There are innumerable renderings of the Ramayana in the Indian languages.

overwhelmed by a flood of rhymes and alliterations.

On some occasions these readings would give rise to shastric discussions, which would at length be settled by the depth of Iswar's wise pronouncements. Though, as one of the children's servants, his rank in our domestic society was below that of many, yet, as with old Grandfather Bhisma in the Mahabharata, his supremacy would assert itself from his seat below his juniors.

Our grave and reverend servitor had one weakness to which, for the sake of historical accuracy, I feel bound to allude. He used to take opium. This created a craving for rich food. So that when he brought us our morning goblets of milk the forces of attraction in his mind would be greater than those of repulsion. If we gave the least expression to our natural repugnance for this meal, no sense of responsibility for our health could prompt him to press it on us a second time.

Iswar also held somewhat narrow views as to our capacity for solid nourishment. We would sit down to our evening repast and a quantity of *luchis*[1] heaped on a thick round wooden tray would be placed before us. He would begin by gingerly dropping a few on each platter, from a

[1] A kind of crisp unsweetened pancake taken like bread along with the other courses.

sufficient height to safeguard himself from contamination[1]—like unwilling favours, wrested from the gods by dint of importunity, did they descend, so dexterously inhospitable was he. Next would come the inquiry whether he should give us any more. I knew the reply which would be most gratifying, and could not bring myself to deprive him by asking for another help.

Then again Iswar was entrusted with a daily allowance of money for procuring our afternoon light refreshment. He would ask us every morning what we should like to have. We knew that to mention the cheapest would be accounted best, so sometimes we ordered a light refection of puffed rice, and at others an indigestible one of boiled gram or roasted groundnuts. It was evident that Iswar was not as painstakingly punctilious in regard to our diet as with the shastric proprieties.

(5) *The Normal School*

While at the Oriental Seminary I had discovered a way out of the degradation of being a mere pupil. I had started a class of my own in a corner of our verandah. The wooden bars of the railing

[1] Food while being eaten, and utensils or anything else touched by the hand engaged in conveying food to the mouth, are considered ceremonially unclean.

were my pupils, and I would act the schoolmaster, cane in hand, seated on a chair in front of them. I had decided which were the good boys and which the bad—nay, further, I could distinguish clearly the quiet from the naughty, the clever from the stupid. The bad rails had suffered so much from my constant caning that they must have longed to give up the ghost had they been alive. And the more scarred they got with my strokes the worse they angered me, till I knew not how to punish them enough. None remain to bear witness to-day how tremendously I tyrannised over that poor dumb class of mine. My wooden pupils have since been replaced by cast-iron railings, nor have any of the new generation taken up their education in the same way—they could never have made the same impression.

I have since realised how much easier it is to acquire the manner than the matter. Without an effort had I assimilated all the impatience, the short temper, the partiality and the injustice displayed by my teachers to the exclusion of the rest of their teaching. My only consolation is that I had not the power of venting these barbarities on any sentient creature. Nevertheless the difference between my wooden pupils and those of the Seminary did not prevent my psychology from being identical with that of its schoolmasters.

I could not have been long at the Oriental Seminary, for I was still of tender age when I joined the Normal School. The only one of its features which I remember is that before the classes began all the boys had to sit in a row in the gallery and go through some kind of singing or chanting of verses—evidently an attempt at introducing an element of cheerfulness into the daily routine.

Unfortunately the words were English and the tune quite as foreign, so that we had not the faintest notion what sort of incantation we were practising; neither did the meaningless monotony of the performance tend to make us cheerful. This failed to disturb the serene self-satisfaction of the school authorities at having provided such a treat; they deemed it superfluous to inquire into the practical effect of their bounty; they would probably have counted it a crime for the boys not to be dutifully happy. Anyhow they rested content with taking the song as they found it, words and all, from the self-same English book which had furnished the theory.

The language into which this English resolved itself in our mouths cannot but be edifying to philologists. I can recall only one line:

Kallokee pullokee singill mellaling mellaling mellaling.

After much thought I have been able to guess

at the original of a part of it. Of what words *kallokee* is the transformation still baffles me. The rest I think was:

. . . *full of glee, singing merrily, merrily, merrily!*

As my memories of the Normal School emerge from haziness and become clearer they are not the least sweet in any particular. Had I been able to associate with the other boys, the woes of learning might not have seemed so intolerable. But that turned out to be impossible—so nasty were most of the boys in their manners and habits. So, in the intervals of the classes, I would go up to the second storey and while away the time sitting near a window overlooking the street. I would count: one year—two years—three years—; wondering how many such would have to be got through like this.

Of the teachers I remember only one, whose language was so foul that, out of sheer contempt for him, I steadily refused to answer any one of his questions. Thus I sat silent throughout the year at the bottom of his class, and while the rest of the class was busy I would be left alone to attempt the solution of many an intricate problem.

One of these, I remember, on which I used to cogitate profoundly, was how to defeat an enemy without having arms. My preoccupation with this question, amidst the hum of the boys reciting their lessons, comes back to me even now. If I could properly train up a number of dogs, tigers and other ferocious beasts, and put a few lines of these on the field of battle, that, I thought, would serve very well as an inspiriting prelude. With our personal prowess let loose thereafter, victory should by no means be out of reach. And, as the picture of this wonderfully simple strategy waxed vivid in my imagination, the victory of my side became assured beyond doubt.

While work had not yet come into my life I always found it easy to devise short cuts to achievement; since I have been working I find that what is hard is hard indeed, and what is difficult remains difficult. This, of course, is less comforting; but nowhere near so bad as the discomfort of trying to take shortcuts.

When at length a year of that class had passed, we were examined in Bengali by Pandit Madhusudan Vachaspati. I got the largest number of marks of all the boys. The teacher complained to the school authorities that there had been favouritism in my case. So I was examined a second time, with the superintendent of the school seated beside the examiner. This time, also, I got a top place.

(6) *Versification*

I could not have been more than eight years old at the time. Jyoti, a son of a niece of my father's, was considerably older than I. He had just gained an entrance into English literature, and would recite Hamlet's soliloquy with great gusto. Why he should have taken it into his head to get a child, as I was, to write poetry I cannot tell. One afternoon he sent for me to his room, and asked me to try and make up a verse; after which he explained to me the construction of the *payar* metre of fourteen syllables.

I had up to then only seen poems in printed books—no mistakes penned through, no sign to the eye of doubt or trouble or any human weakness. I could not have dared even to imagine that any effort of mine could produce such poetry.

One day a thief had been caught in our house. Overpowered by curiosity, yet in fear and trembling, I ventured to the spot to take a peep at him. I found he was just an ordinary man! And when he was somewhat roughly handled by our doorkeeper I felt a great pity. I had a similar experience with poetry.

When, after stringing together a few words at my own sweet will, I found them turned into a *payar* verse I felt I had no illusions left about the glories of poetising. So when poor Poetry is mishandled, even now I feel as unhappy as I did about the thief. Many a time have I been moved to pity and yet been unable to restrain impatient hands itching for the assault. Thieves have scarcely suffered so much, and from so many.

The first feeling of awe once overcome there was no holding me back. I managed to get hold of a blue-paper manuscript book by the favour of one of the officers of our estate. With my own hands I ruled it with pencil lines, at not very regular intervals, and thereon I began to write verses in a large childish scrawl.

Like a young deer which butts here, there and everywhere with its newly sprouting horns, I made myself a nuisance with my budding poetry. More so my elder [1] brother, whose pride in my performance impelled him to hunt about the house for an audience.

I recollect how, as the pair of us, one day, were coming out of the estate offices on the ground floor, after a conquering expedition against the officers, we came across the editor of "The National Paper," Nabagopal Mitter, who had just stepped into the house. My brother tackled him without

[1] The writer is the youngest of seven brothers. The sixth brother is here meant.

further ado: "Look here, Nabagopal Babu! won't you listen to a poem which Rabi has written?" The reading forthwith followed.

My works had not as yet become voluminous. The poet could carry all his effusions about in his pockets. I was writer, printer and publisher, all in one; my brother, as advertiser, being my only colleague. I had composed some verses on The Lotus which I recited to Nabagopal Babu then and there, at the foot of the stairs, in a voice pitched as high as my enthusiasm. "Well done!" said he with a smile. "But what is a *dwirepha?*"[1]

How I had got hold of this word I do not remember. The ordinary name would have fitted the metre quite as well. But this was the one word in the whole poem on which I had pinned my hopes. It had doubtless duly impressed our officers. But curiously enough Nabagopal Babu did not succumb to it—on the contrary he smiled! He could not be an understanding man, I felt sure. I never read poetry to him again. I have since added many years to my age but have not been able to improve upon my test of what does or does not constitute understanding in my hearer. However Nabagopal Babu might smile, the word *dwirepha*, like a bee drunk with honey. stuck to its place, unmoved.

[1] Obsolete word meaning bee.

(7) *Various Learning*

One of the teachers of the Normal School also gave us private lessons at home. His body was lean, his features dry, his voice sharp. He looked like a cane incarnate. His hours were from six to half-past-nine in the morning. With him our reading ranged from popular literary and science readers in Bengali to the epic of Meghnadvadha.

My third brother was very keen on imparting to us a variety of knowledge. So at home we had to go through much more than what was required by the school course. We had to get up before dawn and, clad in loin-cloths, begin with a bout or two with a blind wrestler. Without a pause we donned our tunics on our dusty bodies, and started on our courses of literature, mathematics, geography and history. On our return from school our drawing and gymnastic masters would be ready for us. In the evening Aghore Babu came for our English lessons. It was only after nine that we were free.

On Sunday morning we had singing lessons with Vishnu. Then, almost every Sunday, came Sitanath Dutta to give us demonstrations in physical science. The last were of great interest to me. I remember distinctly the feeling of wonder which filled me when he put some water, with sawdust in it, on the fire in a glass vessel, and showed us how the lightened hot water came up, and the cold water went down and how finally the water began to boil. I also felt a great elation the day I learnt that water is a separable part of milk, and that milk thickens when boiled because the water frees itself as vapour from the connexion. Sunday did not feel Sunday-like unless Sitanath Babu turned up.

There was also an hour when we would be told all about human bones by a pupil of the Campbell Medical School, for which purpose a skeleton, with the bones fastened together by wires was hung up in our schoolroom. And finally, time was also found for Pandit Heramba Tatwaratna to come and get us to learn by rote rules of Sanscrit grammar. I am not sure which of them, the names of the bones or the *sutras* of the grammarian, were the more jaw-breaking. I think the latter took the palm.

We began to learn English after we had made considerable progress in learning through the medium of Bengali. Aghore Babu, our English tutor, was attending the Medical College, so he came to teach us in the evening.

Books tell us that the discovery of fire was one of the biggest discoveries of man. I do not wish to dispute this. But I cannot help feeling how fortunate the little birds are that their parents cannot light lamps of an evening. They have their language lessons early in the morning and you must have noticed how gleefully they learn them. Of course we must not forget that they do not have to learn the English language!

The health of this medical-student tutor of ours was so good that even the fervent and united wishes of his three pupils were not enough to cause his absence even for a day. Only once was he laid up with a broken head when, on the occasion of a fight between the Indian and Eurasian students of the Medical College, a chair was thrown at him. It was a regrettable occurrence; nevertheless we were not able to take it as a personal sorrow, and his recovery somehow seemed to us needlessly swift.

It is evening. The rain is pouring in lance-like showers. Our lane is under knee-deep water. The tank has overflown into the garden, and the bushy tops of the Bael trees are seen standing out over the waters. Our whole being, on this delightful rainy evening, is radiating rapture like the *Kadamba* flower its fragrant spikes. The time for the arrival of our tutor is over by just a few minutes. Yet there is no certainty. . . ! We are sitting on the verandah overlooking the lane[1] watching and watching with a piteous gaze. All of a sudden, with a great big thump, our hearts seem to fall in a swoon. The familiar black umbrella has turned the corner undefeated even by such weather! Could it not be somebody else? It certainly could not! In the wide wide world there might be found another, his equal in pertinacity, but never in this little lane of ours.

Looking back on his period as a whole, I cannot say that Aghore Babu was a hard man. He did not rule us with a rod. Even his rebukes did not amount to scoldings. But whatever may have been his personal merits, his time was *evening*, and his subject *English!* I am certain that even an angel would have seemed a veritable messenger of Yama[2] to any Bengali boy if he came to him at the end of his miserable day at school, and lighted a dismally dim lamp to teach him English.

How well do I remember the day our tutor tried to impress on us the attractiveness of the English language. With this object he recited to us with great unction some lines—prose or poetry we could not tell—out of an English book. It had a most unlooked for effect on us. We laughed so im-

[1] The lane, a blind one, leads, at right angles to the front verandah, from the public main road to the grounds round the house.

[2] God of Death.

moderately that he had to dismiss us for that evening. He must have realised that he held no easy brief—that to get us to pronounce in his favour would entail a contest ranging over years.

Aghore Babu would sometimes try to bring the zephyr of outside knowledge to play on the arid routine of our schoolroom. One day he brought a paper parcel out of his pocket and said: "I'll show you to-day a wonderful piece of work of the Creator." With this he untied the paper wrapping and, producing a portion of the vocal organs of a human being, proceeded to expound the marvels of its mechanism.

I can still call to mind the shock this gave me at the time. I had always thought the whole man spoke—had never even imagined that the act of speech could be viewed in this detached way. However wonderful the mechanism of a part may be, it is certainly less so than the whole man. Not that I put it to myself in so many words, but that was the cause of my dismay. It was perhaps because the tutor had lost sight of this truth that the pupil could not respond to the enthusiasm with which he was discoursing on the subject.

Another day he took us to the dissecting room of the Medical College. The body of an old woman was stretched on the table. This did not disturb me so much. But an amputated leg which was lying on the floor upset me altogether. To view man in this fragmentary way seemed to me so horrid, so absurd that I could not get rid of the impression of that dark, unmeaning leg for many a day.

After getting through Peary Sarkar's first and second English readers we entered upon McCulloch's Course of Reading. Our bodies were weary at the end of the day, our minds yearning for the inner apartments, the book was black and thick with difficult words, and the subject-matter could hardly have been more inviting, for in those days, Mother Saraswati's [1] maternal tenderness was not in evidence. Children's books were not full of pictures then as they are now. Moreover, at the gateway of every reading lesson stood sentinel an array of words, with separated syllables, and forbidding accent marks like fixed bayonets, barring the way to the infant mind. I had repeatedly attacked their serried ranks in vain.

Our tutor would try to shame us by recounting the exploits of some other brilliant pupil of his. We felt duly ashamed, and also not well-disposed towards that other pupil, but this did not help to dispel the darkness which clung to that black volume.

[1] Goddess of Learning.

Providence, out of pity for mankind, has instilled a soporific charm into all tedious things. No sooner did our English lessons begin than our heads began to nod. Sprinkling water into our eyes, or taking a run round the verandahs, were palliatives which had no lasting effect. If by any chance my eldest brother happened to be passing that way, and caught a glimpse of our sleep-tormented condition, we would get let off for the rest of the evening. It did not take our drowsiness another moment to get completely cured.

(8) *My First Outing*

Once, when the dengue fever was raging in Calcutta, some portion of our extensive family had to take shelter in Chhatu Babu's river-side villa. We were among them.

This was my first outing. The bank of the Ganges welcomed me into its lap like a friend of a former birth. There, in front of the servants' quarters, was a grove of guava trees; and, sitting in the verandah under the shade of these, gazing at the flowing current through the gaps between their trunks, my days would pass. Every morning, as I awoke, I somehow felt the day coming to me like a new gilt-edged letter, with some unheard-of news awaiting me on the opening of the envelope. And, lest I should lose any fragment of it, I would hurry through my toilet to my chair outside. Every day there was the ebb and flow of the tide on the Ganges; the various gait of so many different boats; the shifting of the shadows of the trees from west to east; and, over the fringe of shade-patches of the woods on the opposite bank, the gush of golden life-blood through the pierced breast of the evening sky. Some days would be cloudy from early morning; the opposite woods black; black shadows moving over the river. Then with a rush would come the vociferous rain, blotting out the horizon; the dim line of the other bank taking its leave in tears: the river swelling with suppressed heavings; and the moist wind making free with the foliage of the trees overhead.

I felt that out of the bowels of wall, beam and rafter, I had a new birth into the outside. In making fresh acquaintance with things, the dingy covering of petty habits seemed to drop off the world. I am sure that the sugar-cane molasses, which I had with cold *luchis* for my breakfast, could not have tasted different from the ambrosia which *Indra* [1] quaffs in his heaven; for, the immortality is not in the nectar but in the taster, and thus is missed by those who seek it.

[1] The Jupiter Pluvius of Hindu Mythology.

Behind the house was a walled-in enclosure with a tank and a flight of steps leading into the water from a bathing platform. On one side of the platform was an immense Jambolan tree, and all round were various fruit trees, growing in thick clusters, in the shade of which the tank nestled in its privacy. The veiled beauty of this retired little inner garden had a wonderful charm for me, so different from the broad expanse of the river-bank in front. It was like the bride of the house, in the seclusion of her midday siesta, resting on a many-coloured quilt of her own embroidering, murmuring low the secrets of her heart. Many a midday hour did I spend alone under that Jambolan tree dreaming of the fearsome kingdom of the Yakshas [1] within the depths of the tank.

I had a great curiosity to see a Bengal village. Its clusters of cottages, its thatched pavilions, its lanes and bathing places, its games and gatherings, its fields and markets, its life as a whole as I saw it in imagination, greatly attracted me. Just such a village was right on the other side of our garden wall, but it was forbidden to us. We had come out, but not into freedom. We had been in a cage, and were now on a perch, but the chain was still there.

[1] The King of the Yakshas is the Pluto of Hindu Mythology.

One morning two of our elders went out for a stroll into the village. I could not restrain my eagerness any longer, and, slipping out unperceived, followed them for some distance. As I went along the deeply shaded lane, with its close thorny *seora* hedges, by the side of the tank covered with green water weeds, I rapturously took in picture after picture. I still remember the man with bare body, engaged in a belated toilet on the edge of the tank, cleaning his teeth with the chewed end of a twig. Suddenly my elders became aware of my presence behind them. "Get away, get away, go back at once!" they scolded. They were scandalised. My feet were bare, I had no scarf or upper-robe over my tunic, I was not dressed fit to come out; as if it was my fault! I never owned any socks or superfluous apparel, so not only went back disappointed for that morning, but had no chance of repairing my shortcomings and being allowed to come out any other day. However though the Beyond was thus shut out from behind, in front the Ganges freed me from all bondage, and my mind, whenever it listed, could embark on the boats gaily sailing along, and hie away to lands not named in any geography.

This was forty years ago. Since then I have never set foot again in that *champak*-shaded villa garden. The same old house and the same old trees must still be there, but I know it cannot any longer be the same—for where am I now to get that fresh feeling of wonder which made it what it was?

We returned to our Jorasanko house in town. And my days were as so many mouthfuls offered up to be gulped down into the yawning interior of the Normal School.

(9) *Practising Poetry*

That blue manuscript book was soon filled, like the hive of some insect, with a network of variously slanting lines and the thick and thin strokes of letters. The eager pressure of the boy writer soon crumpled its leaves; and then the edges got frayed, and twisted up claw-like as if to hold fast the writing within, till at last, down what river *Baitarani* [1] I know not, its pages were swept away by merciful oblivion. Anyhow they escaped the pangs of a passage through the printing press and need fear no birth into this vale of woe.

I cannot claim to have been a passive witness of the spread of my reputation as a poet. Though Satkari Babu was not a teacher of our class he

[1] Corresponding to Lethe.

was very fond of me. He had written a book on Natural History—wherein I hope no unkind humorist will try to find a reason for such fondness. He sent for me one day and asked: "So you write poetry, do you?" I did not conceal the fact. From that time on, he would now and then ask me to complete a quatrain by adding a couplet of my own to one given by him.

Gobinda Babu of our school was very dark, and short and fat. He was the Superintendent. He sat, in his black suit, with his account books, in an office room on the second storey. We were all afraid of him, for he was the rod-bearing judge. On one occasion I had escaped from the attentions of some bullies into his room. The persecutors were five or six older boys. I had no one to bear witness on my side—except my tears. I won my case and since then Govinda Babu had a soft corner in his heart for me.

One day he called me into his room during the recess. I went in fear and trembling but had no sooner stepped before him than he also accosted me with the question: "So you write poetry?" I did not hesitate to make the admission. He commissioned me to write a poem on some high moral precept which I do not remember. The amount of condescension and affability which such a request coming from him implied can only be appreciated by those who were his pupils. When I finished and handed him the verses next day, he took me to the highest class and made me stand before the boys. "Recite," he commanded. And I recited loudly.

The only praiseworthy thing about this moral poem was that it soon got lost. Its moral effect on that class was far from encouraging—the sentiment it aroused being not one of regard for its author. Most of them were certain that it was not my own composition. One said he could produce the book from which it was copied, but was not pressed to do so; the process of proving is such a nuisance to those who want to believe. Finally the number of seekers after poetic fame began to increase alarmingly; moreover their methods were not those which are recognised as roads to moral improvement.

Nowadays there is nothing strange in a youngster writing verses. The glamour of poesy is gone. I remember how the few women who wrote poetry in those days were looked upon as miraculous creations of the Deity. If one hears to-day that some young lady does not write poems one feels sceptical. Poetry now sprouts long before the highest Bengali class is reached; so that no modern Gobinda Babu would have taken any notice of the poetic exploit I have recounted.

PART III

(10) *Srikantha Babu*

AT this time I was blessed with a hearer the like of whom I shall never get again. He had so inordinate a capacity for being pleased as to have utterly disqualified him for the post of critic in any of our monthly Reviews. The old man was like a perfectly ripe Alfonso mango—not a trace of acid or coarse fibre in his composition. His tender clean-shaven face was rounded off by an all-pervading baldness; there was not the vestige of a tooth to worry the inside of his mouth; and his big smiling eyes gleamed with a constant delight. When he spoke in his soft deep voice, his mouth and eyes and hands all spoke likewise. He was of the old school of Persian culture and knew not a word of English. His inseparable companions were a hubble-bubble at his left, and a *sitar* on his lap; and from his throat flowed song unceasing.

Srikantha Babu had no need to wait for a formal introduction, for none could resist the natural claims of his genial heart. Once he took us to be photographed with him in some big English photographic studio. There he so captivated the proprietor with his artless story, in a jumble of Hindusthani and Bengali, of how he was a poor man, but badly wanted this particular photograph taken, that the man smilingly allowed him a reduced rate. Nor did such bargaining sound at all incongruous in that unbending English establishment, so naïve was Srikantha Babu, so unconscious of any possibility of giving offence. He would sometimes take me along to a European missionary's house. There, also, with his playing and singing, his caresses of the missionary's little girl and his unstinted admiration of the little booted feet of the missionary's lady, he would enliven the gathering as no one else could have done. Another behaving so absurdly would have been deemed a bore, but his transparent simplicity pleased all and drew them to join in his gaiety.

Srikantha Babu was impervious to rudeness or insolence. There was at the time a singer of some repute retained in our establishment. When the latter was the worse for liquor he would rail at poor Srikantha Babu's singing in no very choice terms. This he would bear unflinchingly, with no attempt at retort. When at last the man's incorrigible rudeness brought about his dismissal Srikantha Babu anxiously interceded for him. "It was not he, it was the liquor," he insisted.

He could not bear to see anyone sorrowing or even to hear of it. So when any one of the boys wanted to torment him they had only to read

The Ganges

out passages from Vidyasagar's "Banishment of Sita"; whereat he would be greatly exercised, thrusting out his hands in protest and begging and praying of them to stop.

This old man was the friend alike of my father, my elder brothers and ourselves. He was of an age with each and every one of us. As any piece of stone is good enough for the freshet to dance round and gambol with, so the least provocation would suffice to make him beside himself with joy. Once I had composed a hymn, and had not failed to make due allusion to the trials and tribulations of this world. Srikantha Babu was convinced that my father would be overjoyed at such a perfect gem of a devotional poem. With unbounded enthusiasm he volunteered personally to acquaint him with it. By a piece of good fortune I was not there at the time but heard afterwards that my father was hugely amused that the sorrows of the world should have so early moved his youngest son to the point of versification. I am sure Gobinda Babu, the superintendent, would have shown more respect for my effort on so serious a subject.

In singing I was Srikantha Babu's favorite pupil. He had taught me a song: "No more of Vraja[1] for me," and would drag me about to

[1] Krishna's playground.

everyone's rooms and get me to sing it to them. I would sing and he would thrum an accompaniment on his *sitar* and when we came to the chorus he would join in, and repeat it over and over again, smiling and nodding his head at each one in turn, as if nudging them on to a more enthusiastic appreciation.

He was a devoted admirer of my father. A hymn had been set to one of his tunes, "For He is the heart of our hearts." When he sang this to my father Srikantha Babu got so excited that he jumped up from his seat and in alternation violently twanged his *sitar* as he sang: "For He is the heart of our hearts" and then waved his hand about my father's face as he changed the words to "For *you* are the heart of our hearts."

When the old man paid his last visit to my father, the latter, himself bed-ridden, was at a river-side villa in Chinsurah. Srikantha Babu, stricken with his last illness, could not rise unaided and had to push open his eyelids to see. In this state, tended by his daughter, he journeyed to Chinsurah from his place in Birbhoom. With a great effort he managed to take the dust of my father's feet and then return to his lodgings in Chinsurah where he breathed his last a few days later. I heard afterwards from his daughter that he went to his eternal youth with the song "How sweet is thy mercy, Lord!" on his lips.

(11) *Our Bengali Course Ends*

At School we were then in the class below the highest one. At home we had advanced in Bengali much further than the subjects taught in the class. We had been through Akshay Datta's book on Popular Physics, and had also finished the epic of Meghnadvadha. We read our physics without any reference to physical objects and so our knowledge of the subject was correspondingly bookish. In fact the time spent on it had been thoroughly wasted; much more so to my mind than if it had been wasted in doing nothing. The Meghnadvadha, also, was not a thing of joy to us. The tastiest tit-bit may not be relished when thrown at one's head. To employ an epic to teach language is like using a sword to shave with—sad for the sword, bad for the chin. A poem should be taught from the emotional standpoint; inveigling it into service as grammar-cum-dictionary is not calculated to propitiate the divine Saraswati.

All of a sudden our Normal School career came to an end; and thereby hangs a tale. One of our school teachers wanted to borrow a copy of my grandfather's life by Mitra from our library. My nephew and classmate Satya managed to screw up courage enough to volunteer to mention this to my father. He came to the conclusion that everyday Bengali would hardly do to approach him with. So he concocted and delivered himself of an archaic phrase with such meticulous precision that my father must have felt our study of the Bengali language had gone a bit too far and was in danger of over-reaching itself. So the next morning, when according to our wont our table had been placed in the south verandah, the blackboard hung up on a nail in the wall, and everything was in readiness for our lessons with Nilkamal Babu, we three were sent for by my father to his room upstairs. "You need not do any more Bengali lessons," he said. Our minds danced for very joy.

Nilkamal Babu was waiting downstairs, our books were lying open on the table, and the idea of getting us once more to go through the Meghnadvadha doubtless still occupied his mind. But as on one's death-bed the various routine of daily life seems unreal, so, in a moment, did everything, from the Pandit down to the nail on which the blackboard was hung, become for us as empty as a mirage. Our sole trouble was how to give this news to Nilkamal Babu with due decorum.

We did it at last with considerable restraint, while the geometrical figures on the blackboard stared at us in wonder and the blank verse of the Meghnadvadha looked blankly on.

Our Pandit's parting words were: "At the call of duty I may have been sometimes harsh with you—do not keep that in remembrance. You will learn the value of what I have taught you later on."

Indeed I have learnt that value. It was because we were taught in our own language that our minds quickened. Learning should as far as possible follow the process of eating. When the taste begins from the first bite, the stomach is awakened to its function before it is loaded, so that its digestive juices get full play. Nothing like this happens, however, when the Bengali boy is taught in English. The first bite bids fair to wrench loose both rows of teeth—like a veritable earthquake in the mouth! And by the time he discovers that the morsel is not of the genus stone, but a digestible bonbon, half his allotted span of life is over. While one is choking and spluttering over the spelling and grammar, the inside remains starved, and when at length the taste is felt, the appetite has vanished. If the whole mind does not work from the beginning its full powers remain undeveloped to the end. While all around was the cry for English teaching, my third brother was brave enough to keep us to our Bengali course. To him in heaven my grateful reverence.

(12) *The Professor*

On leaving the Normal School we were sent to the Bengal Academy, a Eurasian institution. We felt we had gained an access of dignity, that we had grown up—at least into the first storey of freedom. In point of fact the only progress we made in that academy was towards freedom. What we were taught there we never understood, nor did we make any attempt to learn, nor did it seem to make any difference to anybody that we did not. The boys here were annoying but not disgusting—which was a great comfort. They wrote ASS on their palms and slapped it on to our backs with a cordial "hello!" They gave us a dig in the ribs from behind and looked innocently another way. They dabbed banana pulp on our heads and made away unperceived. Nevertheless it was like coming out of slime on to rock—we were worried but not soiled.

This school had one great advantage for me. No one there cherished the forlorn hope that boys of our sort could make any advance in learning. It was a petty institution with an insufficient income, so that we had one supreme merit in the eyes of its authorities—we paid our fees regularly. This prevented even the Latin Grammar from proving a stumbling block, and the most egregious of blunders left our backs unscathed. Pity for us had nothing to do with it—the school authorities had spoken to the teachers!

Still, harmless though it was, after all it was a school. The rooms were cruelly dismal with their walls on guard like policemen. The house was more like a pigeon-holed box than a human habitation. No decoration, no pictures, not a touch of colour, not an attempt to attract the boyish heart. The fact that likes and dislikes form a large part of the child mind was completely ignored. Naturally our whole being was depressed as we stepped through its doorway into the narrow quadrangle—and playing truant became chronic with us.

In this we found an accomplice. My elder brothers had a Persian tutor. We used to call him Munshi. He was of middle age and all skin and bone, as though dark parchment had been stretched over his skeleton without any filling of flesh and blood. He probably knew Persian well, his knowledge of English was quite fair, but in neither of these directions lay his ambition. His belief was that his proficiency in singlestick was matched only by his skill in song. He would stand in the sun in the middle of our courtyard and go through a wonderful series of antics with a staff—his own shadow being his antagonist. I need hardly add that his shadow never got the better of him and when at the end he gave a great big shout and whacked it on the head with a victorious smile, it lay submissively prone at his feet. His singing, nasal and out of tune, sounded like a gruesome mixture of groaning and moaning coming from some ghost-world. Our singing master Vishnu would sometimes chaff him: "Look here, Munshi, you'll be taking the bread out of our mouths at this rate!" To which his only reply would be a disdainful smile.

This shows that the Munshi was amenable to soft words; and in fact, whenever we wanted we could persuade him to write to the school authorities to excuse us from attendance. The school authorities took no pains to scrutinise these letters, they knew it would be all the same whether we attended or not, so far as educational results were concerned.

I have now a school of my own in which the boys are up to all kinds of mischief, for boys will be mischievous—and schoolmasters unforgiving. When any of us are beset with undue uneasiness at their conduct and are stirred into a resolution to deal out condign punishment, the misdeeds of my own schooldays confront me in a row and smile at me.

I now clearly see that the mistake is to judge boys by the standard of grown-ups, to forget that a child is quick and mobile like a running stream; and that, in the case of such, any touch of imperfection need cause no great alarm, for the speed of the flow is itself the best corrective. When stagnation sets in then comes the danger. So it is for the teacher, more than the pupil, to beware of wrongdoing.

There was a separate refreshment room for Bengali boys for meeting their caste requirements. This was where we struck up a friendship with some of the others. They were all older than we. One of these will bear to be dilated upon.

His specialty was the art of Magic, so much so that he had actually written and published a little booklet on it, the front page of which bore his name with the title of Professor. I had never before come across a schoolboy whose name had appeared in print, so that my reverence for him—as a professor of magic I mean—was profound. How could I have brought myself to believe that anything questionable could possibly find place in the straight and upright ranks of printed letters? To be able to record one's own words in indelible ink—was that a slight thing? To stand unscreened yet unabashed, self-confessed before the world,—how could one withhold belief in the face of such supreme self-confidence? I remember how once I got the types for the letters of my name from some printing press, and what a memorable thing it seemed when I inked and pressed them on paper and found my name imprinted.

We used to give a lift in our carriage to this schoolfellow and author-friend of ours. This led to visiting terms. He was also great at theatricals. With his help we erected a stage on our wrestling ground with painted paper stretched over a split bamboo framework. But a peremptory negative from upstairs prevented any play from being acted thereon.

A comedy of errors was however played later on without any stage at all. The author of this has already been introduced to the reader in these pages. He was none other than my nephew Satya. Those who behold his present calm and sedate demeanour would be shocked to learn of the tricks of which he was the originator.

The event of which I am writing happened sometime afterwards when I was twelve or thirteen. Our magician friend had told of so many strange properties of things that I was consumed with curiosity to see them for myself. But the

Satya

materials of which he spoke were invariably so rare or distant that one could hardly hope to get hold of them without the help of Sindbad the sailor. Once, as it happened, the Professor forgot himself so far as to mention accessible things. Who could ever believe that a seed dipped and dried twenty-one times in the juice of a species of cactus would sprout and flower and fruit all in the space of an hour? I was determined to test this, not daring withal to doubt the assurance of a Professor whose name appeared in a printed book.

I got our gardener to furnish me with a plentiful supply of the milky juice, and betook myself, on a Sunday afternoon, to our mystic nook in a corner of the roof terrace, to experiment with the stone of a mango. I was wrapt in my task of dipping and drying—but the grown-up reader will probably not wait to ask me the result. In the meantime, I little knew that Satya, in another corner, had, in the space of an hour, caused to root and sprout a mystical plant of his own creation. This was to bear curious fruit later on.

After the day of this experiment the Professor rather avoided me, as I gradually came to perceive. He would not sit on the same side in the carriage, and altogether seemed to fight shy of me.

One day, all of a sudden, he proposed that each one in turn should jump off the bench in our schoolroom. He wanted to observe the differences in style, he said. Such scientific curiosity did not appear queer in a professor of magic. Everyone jumped, so did I. He shook his head with a subdued "h'm." No amount of persuasion could draw anything further out of him.

Another day he informed us that some good friends of his wanted to make our acquaintance and asked us to accompany him to their house. Our guardians had no objection, so off we went. The crowd in the room seemed full of curiosity. They expressed their eagerness to hear me sing. I sang a song or two. Mere child as I was I could hardly have bellowed like a bull. "Quite a sweet voice," they all agreed.

When refreshments were put before us they sat round and watched us eat. I was bashful by nature and not used to strange company; moreover the habit I acquired during the attendance of our servant Iswar left me a poor eater for good. They all seemed impressed with the delicacy of my appetite.

In the fifth act I got some curiously warm letters from our Professor which revealed the whole situation. And here let the curtain fall.

I subsequently learnt from Satya that while I had been practising magic on the mango seed, he had successfully convinced the Professor that I was dressed as a boy by our guardians merely for getting me a better schooling, but that really this was only a disguise. To those who are curious in regard to imaginary science I should explain that a girl is supposed to jump with her left foot forward, and this is what I had done on the occasion of the Professor's trial. I little realised at the time what a tremendously false step mine had been!

(13) *My Father*

Shortly after my birth my father took to constantly travelling about. So it is no exaggeration to say that in my early childhood I hardly knew him. He would now and then come back home all of a sudden, and with him came foreign servants with whom I felt extremely eager to make friends. Once there came in this way a young Panjabi servant named Lenu. The cordiality of the reception he got from us would have been worthy of Ranjit Singh himself. Not only was he a foreigner, but a Panjabi to boot,—what wonder he stole our hearts away?

We had the same reverence for the whole Panjabi nation as for Bhima and Arjuna of the Mahabharata. They were warriors; and if they had sometimes fought and lost, that was clearly the enemy's fault. It was glorious to have Lenu, of the Panjab, in our very home.

My sister-in-law had a model war-ship under a glass case, which, when wound up, rocked on blue-painted silken waves to the tinkling of a musical box. I would beg hard for the loan of this to display its marvels to the admiring Lenu.

Caged in the house as we were, anything savouring of foreign parts had a peculiar charm for me. This was one of the reasons why I made so much of Lenu. This was also the reason why Gabriel, the Jew, with his embroidered gaberdine, who came to sell *attars* and scented oils, stirred me so; and the huge Kabulis, with their dusty, baggy trousers and knapsacks and bundles, wrought on my young mind a fearful fascination.

Anyhow, when my father came, we would be content with wandering round about his entourage and in the company of his servants. We did not reach his immediate presence.

Once while my father was away in the Himalayas, that old bogey of the British Government, the Russian invasion, came to be a subject of agitated conversation among the people. Some well-meaning lady friend had enlarged on the impending danger to my mother with all the circumstance of a prolific imagination. How could a body tell from which of the Tibetan passes the Russian host might suddenly flash forth like a baleful comet?

My mother was seriously alarmed. Possibly the other members of the family did not share her misgivings; so, despairing of grown-up sympathy, she sought my boyish support. "Won't you write to your father about the Russians?" she asked.

That letter, carrying the tidings of my mother's anxieties, was my first one to my father. I did not know how to begin or end a letter, or anything at all about it. I went to Mahananda, the estate munshi.[1] The resulting style of address was doubtless correct enough, but the sentiments could not have escaped the musty flavour inseparable from literature emanating from an estate office.

I got a reply to my letter. My father asked me not to be afraid; if the Russians came he would drive them away himself. This confident assurance did not seem to have the effect of relieving my mother's fears, but it served to free me from all timidity as regards my father. After that I wanted to write to him every day and pestered Mahananda accordingly. Unable to withstand my importunity he would make out drafts for me to copy. But I did not know that there was the postage to be paid for. I had an idea that letters placed in Mahananda's hands got to their destina-

[1] Correspondence clerk.

tion without any need for further worry. It is hardly necessary to mention that, Mahananda being considerably older than myself, these letters never reached the Himalayan hill-tops.

When, after his long absences, my father came home even for a few days, the whole house seemed filled with the weight of his presence. We would see our elders at certain hours, formally robed in their *chogas*, passing to his rooms with restrained gait and sobered mien, casting away any *pan*[1] they might have been chewing. Everyone seemed on the alert. To make sure of nothing going wrong, my mother would superintend the cooking herself. The old mace-bearer, Kinu, with his white livery and crested turban, on guard at my father's door, would warn us not to be boisterous in the verandah in front of his rooms during his midday siesta. We had to walk past quietly, talking in whispers, and dared not even take a peep inside.

On one occasion my father came home to invest the three of us with the sacred thread. With the help of Pandit Vedantavagish he had collected the old Vedic rites for the purpose. For days together we were taught to chant in correct accents the selections from the Upanishads, arranged by my father under the name of "Brahma Dharma," seated in the prayer hall with Becharam Babu.

[1] Spices wrapped in betel leaf.

Finally, with shaven heads and gold rings in our ears, we three budding Brahmins went into a three-days' retreat in a portion of the third storey.

It was great fun. The earrings gave us a good handle to pull each other's ears with. We found a little drum lying in one of the rooms; taking this we would stand out in the verandah, and, when we caught sight of any servant passing alone in the storey below, we would rap a tattoo on it. This would make the man look up, only to beat a hasty retreat the next moment with averted eyes.[1] In short we cannot claim that these days of our retirement were passed in ascetic meditation.

I am however persuaded that boys like ourselves could not have been rare in the hermitages of old. And if some ancient document has it that the ten or twelve-year old Saradwata or Sarngarava [2] is spending the whole of the days of his boyhood offering oblations and chanting *mantras*, we are not compelled to put unquestioning faith in the statement; because the book of Boy Nature is even older and also more authentic.

After we had attained full brahminhood I be-

[1] It is considered sinful for non-brahmins to cast glances on neophytes during the process of their sacred-thread investiture, before the ceremony is complete.

[2] Two novices in the hermitage of the sage Kanva, mentioned in the Sanskrit drama, Sakuntala.

came very keen on repeating the *gayatri*.[1] I would meditate on it with great concentration. It is hardly a text the full meaning of which I could have grasped at that age. I well remember what efforts I made to extend the range of my consciousness with the help of the initial invocation of "Earth, firmament and heaven." How I felt or thought it is difficult to express clearly, but this much is certain that to be clear about the meaning of words is not the most important function of the human understanding.

The main object of teaching is not to explain meanings, but to knock at the door of the mind. If any boy is asked to give an account of what is awakened in him at such knocking, he will probably say something very silly. For what happens within is much bigger than what he can express in words. Those who pin their faith on University examinations as a test of all educational results take no account of this fact.

I can recollect many things which I did not understand, but which stirred me deeply. Once, on the roof terrace of our river-side villa, my eldest brother, at the sudden gathering of clouds, repeated aloud some stanzas from Kalidas's "Cloud Messenger." I could not, nor had I the need to, understand a word of the Sanskrit. His ecstatic dec-

[1] The text for self-realisation.

lamation of the sonorous rhythm was enough for me.

Then, again, before I could properly understand English, a profusely illustrated edition of "The Old Curiosity Shop" fell into my hands. I went through the whole of it, though at least nine-tenths of the words were unknown to me. Yet, with the vague ideas I conjured up from the rest, I spun out a variously coloured thread on which to string the illustrations. Any university examiner would have given me a great big zero, but the reading of the book had not proved for me quite so empty as all that.

Another time I had accompanied my father on a trip on the Ganges in his houseboat. Among the books he had with him was an old Fort William edition of Jayadeva's *Gita Govinda.* It was in the Bengali character. The verses were not printed in separate lines, but ran on like prose. I did not then know anything of Sanskrit, yet because of my knowledge of Bengali many of the words were familiar. I cannot tell how often I read that *Gita Govinda.* I can well remember this line:

> The night that was passed in the lonely forest cottage.

It spread an atmosphere of vague beauty over my mind. That one Sanskrit word, Nibhritanikunja-griham, meaning "the lonely forest cottage" was quite enough for me.

I had to discover for myself the intricate metre of Jayadeva, because its divisions were lost in the clumsy prose form of the book. And this discovery gave me very great delight. Of course I did not fully comprehend Jayadeva's meaning. It would hardly be correct to aver that I had got it even partly. But the sound of the words and the lilt of the metre filled my mind with pictures of wonderful beauty, which impelled me to copy out the whole of the book for my own use.

The same thing happened, when I was a little older, with a verse from Kalidas's "Birth of the War God." The verse moved me greatly, though the only words of which I gathered the sense, were "the breeze carrying the spray-mist of the falling waters of the sacred Mandakini and shaking the deodar leaves." These left me pining to taste the beauties of the whole. When, later, a Pandit explained to me that in the next two lines the breeze went on "splitting the feathers of the peacock plume on the head of the eager deer-hunter," the thinness of this last conceit disappointed me. I was much better off when I had relied only upon my imagination to complete the verse.

Whoever goes back to his early childhood will

agree that his greatest gains were not in proportion to the completeness of his understanding. Our Kathakas [1] know this truth well. So their narratives always have a good proportion of ear-filling Sanskrit words and abstruse remarks not calculated to be fully understood by their simple hearers, but only to be suggestive.

The value of such suggestion is by no means to be despised by those who measure education in terms of material gains and losses. These insist on trying to sum up the account and find out exactly how much of the lesson imparted can be rendered up. But children, and those who are not over-educated, dwell in that primal paradise where men can come to know without fully comprehending each step. And only when that paradise is lost comes the evil day when everything needs must be understood. The road which leads to knowledge, without going through the dreary process of understanding, that is the royal road. If that be barred, though the world's marketing may yet go on as usual, the open sea and the mountain top cease to be possible of access.

So, as I was saying, though at that age I could not realise the full meaning of the *Gayatri*, there was something in me which could do without a complete understanding. I am reminded of a day

[1] Bards or reciters.

when, as I was seated on the cement floor in a corner of our schoolroom meditating on the text, my eyes overflowed with tears. Why those tears came I knew not; and to a strict cross-questioner I would probably have given some explanation having nothing to do with the *Gayatri*. The fact of the matter is that what is going on in the inner recesses of consciousness is not always known to the dweller on the surface.

(14) *A journey with my Father*

My shaven head after the sacred thread ceremony caused me one great anxiety. However partial Eurasian lads may be to things appertaining to the Cow, their reverence for the Brahmin [1] is notoriously lacking. So that, apart from other missiles, our shaven heads were sure to be pelted with jeers. While I was worrying over this possibility I was one day summoned upstairs to my father. How would I like to go with him to the Himalayas, I was asked. Away from the Bengal Academy and off to the Himalayas! Would I like it? O that I could have rent the skies with a shout, that might have given some idea of the How!

On the day of our leaving home my father, as

[1] The Cow and the Brahmin are watchwords of modern Hindu Orthodoxy.

was his habit, assembled the whole family in the prayer hall for divine service. After I had taken the dust of the feet of my elders I got into the carriage with my father. This was the first time in my life that I had a full suit of clothes made for me. My father himself had selected the pattern and colour. A gold embroidered velvet cap completed my costume. This I carried in my hand, being assailed with misgivings as to its effect in juxtaposition to my hairless head. As I got into the carriage my father insisted on my wearing it, so I had to put it on. Every time he looked another way I took it off. Every time I caught his eye it had to resume its proper place.

My father was very particular in all his arrangements and orderings. He disliked leaving things vague or undetermined and never allowed slovenliness or makeshifts. He had a well-defined code to regulate his relations with others and theirs with him. In this he was different from the generality of his countrymen. With the rest of us a little carelessness this way or that did not signify; so in our dealings with him we had to be anxiously careful. It was not so much the little less or more that he objected to as the failure to be up to the standard.

My father had also a way of picturing to himself every detail of what he wanted done. On the occasion of any ceremonial gathering, at which he could not be present, he would think out and assign the place for each thing, the duty for each member of the family, the seat for each guest; nothing would escape him. After it was all over he would ask each one for a separate account and thus gain a complete impression of the whole for himself. So, while I was with him on his travels, though nothing would induce him to put obstacles in the way of my amusing myself as I pleased, he left no loophole in the strict rules of conduct which he prescribed for me in other respects.

Our first halt was to be for a few days at Bolpur. Satya had been there a short time before with his parents. No self-respecting nineteenth century infant would have credited the account of his travels which he gave us on his return. But we were different, and had had no opportunity of learning to determine the line between the possible and the impossible. Our Mahabharata and Ramayana gave us no clue to it. Nor had we then any children's illustrated books to guide us in the way a child should go. All the hard and fast laws which govern the world we learnt by knocking up against them.

Satya had told us that, unless one was very very expert, getting into a railway carriage was a terribly dangerous affair—the least slip, and it was all up. Then, again, a fellow had to hold on to his seat with all his might, otherwise the jolt at starting was so tremendous there was no telling where one would get thrown off to. So when we got to the railway station I was all a-quiver. So easily did we get into our compartment, however, that I felt sure the worst was yet to come. And when, at length, we made an absurdly smooth start, without any semblance of adventure, I felt woefully disappointed.

The train sped on; the broad fields with their blue-green border trees, and the villages nestling in their shade flew past in a stream of pictures which melted away like a flood of mirages. It was evening when we reached Bolpur. As I got into the palanquin I closed my eyes. I wanted to preserve the whole of the wonderful vision to be unfolded before my waking eyes in the morning light. The freshness of the experience would be spoilt, I feared, by incomplete glimpses caught in the vagueness of the dusk.

When I woke at dawn my heart was thrilling tremulously as I stepped outside. My predecessor had told me that Bolpur had one feature which was to be found nowhere else in the world. This was the path leading from the main buildings to the servants' quarters which, though not covered over in any way, did not allow a ray of the sun or a drop of rain to touch anybody passing along it. I started to hunt for this wonderful path, but the reader will perhaps not wonder at my failure to find it to this day.

Town bred as I was, I had never seen a rice-field, and I had a charming portrait of the cow-herd boy, of whom we had read, pictured on the canvas of my imagination. I had heard from Satya that the Bolpur house was surrounded by fields of ripening rice, and that playing in these with cowherd boys was an everyday affair, of which the plucking, cooking and eating of the rice was the crowning feature. I eagerly looked about me. But where, oh, where was the rice-field on all that barren heath? Cowherd boys there might have been somewhere about, yet how to distinguish them from any other boys, that was the question!

However it did not take me long to get over what I could not see,—what I did see was quite enough. There was no servant rule here, and the only ring which encircled me was the blue of the horizon which the presiding goddess of these solitudes had drawn round them. Within this I was free to move about as I chose.

Though I was yet a mere child my father did not place any restriction on my wanderings. In the hollows of the sandy soil the rainwater had ploughed deep furrows, carving out miniature mountain ranges full of red gravel and pebbles of various shapes through which ran tiny streams, revealing the geography of Lilliput. From this region I would gather in the lap of my tunic many curious pieces of stone and take the collection to my father. He never made light of my labours. On the contrary he waxed enthusiastic.

"How wonderful!" he exclaimed. "Wherever did you get all these?"

"There are many many more, thousands and thousands!" I burst out. "I could bring as many every day."

"That *would* be nice!" he replied. "Why not decorate my little hill with them?"

An attempt had been made to dig a tank in the garden, but the subsoil water proving too low, it had been abandoned, unfinished, with the excavated earth left piled up into a hillock. On the top of this height my father used to sit for his morning prayer, and as he sat the sun would rise at the edge of the undulating expanse which stretched away to the eastern horizon in front of him. This was the hill he asked me to decorate.

I was very troubled, on leaving Bolpur, that I could not carry away with me my store of stones. It is still difficult for me to realise that I have no absolute claim to keep up a close relationship with things, merely because I have gathered them together. If my fate had granted me the prayer, which I had pressed with such insistence, and undertaken that I should carry this load of stones about with me for ever, then I should scarcely have had the hardihood to laugh at it to-day.

In one of the ravines I came upon a hollow full of spring water which overflowed as a little rivulet, where sported tiny fish battling their way up the current.

"I've found such a lovely spring," I told my father. "Couldn't we get our bathing and drinking water from there?"

"The very thing," he agreed, sharing my rapture, and gave orders for our water supply to be drawn from that spring.

I was never tired of roaming about among those miniature hills and dales in hopes of lighting on something never known before. I was the Livingstone of this undiscovered land which looked as if seen through the wrong end of a telescope. Everything there, the dwarf date palms, the scrubby wild plums and the stunted jambolans, was in keeping with the miniature mountain ranges, the little rivulet and the tiny fish I had discovered.

Singing to My Father

Probably in order to teach me to be careful my father placed a little small change in my charge and required me to keep an account of it. He also entrusted me with the duty of winding his valuable gold watch for him. He overlooked the risk of damage in his desire to train me to a sense of responsibility. When we went out together for our morning walk he would ask me to give alms to any beggars we came across. But I never could render him a proper account at the end of it. One day my balance was larger than the account warranted.

"I really must make you my cashier," observed my father. "Money seems to have a way of growing in your hands!"

That watch of his I wound up with such indefatigable zeal that it had very soon to be sent to the watchmaker's in Calcutta.

I am reminded of the time when, later in life, I was appointed to manage the estate and had to lay before my father, owing to his failing eyesight, a statement of accounts on the second or third of every month. I had first to read out the totals under each head, and if he had any doubts on any point he would ask for the details. If I made any attempt to slur over or keep out of sight any item which I feared he would not like, it was sure to come out. So these first few days of the month were very anxious ones for me.

As I have said, my father had the habit of keeping everything clearly before his mind,—whether figures of accounts, or ceremonial arrangements, or additions or alterations to property. He had never seen the new prayer hall built at Bolpur, and yet he was familiar with every detail of it from questioning those who came to see him after a visit to Bolpur. He had an extraordinary memory, and when once he got hold of a fact it never escaped him.

My father had marked his favourite verses in his copy of the *Bhagavadgita*. He asked me to copy these out, with their translation, for him. At home, I had been a boy of no account, but here, when these important functions were entrusted to me, I felt the glory of the situation.

By this time I was rid of my blue manuscript book and had got hold of a bound volume of one of Lett's diaries. I now saw to it that my poetising should not lack any of the dignity of outward circumstance. It was not only a case of writing poems, but of holding myself forth as a poet before my own imagination. So when I wrote poetry at Bolpur I loved to do it sprawling under a young coconut palm. This seemed to me the true poetic way. Resting thus on the hard unturfed gravel in the burning heat of the day I composed a martial ballad on the "Defeat of King Prithwi." In spite of the superabundance of its martial spirit, it could not escape an early death. That bound volume of Lett's diary has now followed the way of its elder sister, the blue manuscript book, leaving no address behind.

We left Bolpur and making short halts on the way at Sahebganj, Dinapore, Allahabad and Cawnpore we stopped at last at Amritsar.

An incident on the way remains engraved on my memory. The train had stopped at some big station. The ticket examiner came and punched our tickets. He looked at me curiously as if he had some doubt which he did not care to express. He went off and came back with a companion. Both of them fidgetted about for a time near the door of our compartment and then again retired. At last came the station master himself. He looked at my half-ticket and then asked:

"Is not the boy over twelve?"

"No," said my father.

I was then only eleven, but looked older than my age.

"You must pay the full fare for him," said the station master.

My father's eyes flashed as, without a word, he took out a currency note from his box and handed it to the station master. When they brought my father his change he flung it disdainfully back at them, while the station master stood abashed at this exposure of the meanness of his implied doubt.

The golden temple of Amritsar comes back to me like a dream. Many a morning have I accompanied my father to this *Gurudarbar* of the Sikhs in the middle of the lake. There the sacred chanting resounds continually. My father, seated amidst the throng of worshippers, would sometimes add his voice to the hymn of praise, and finding a stranger joining in their devotions they would wax enthusiastically cordial, and we would return loaded with the sanctified offerings of sugar crystals and other sweets.

One day my father invited one of the chanting choir to our place and got him to sing us some of their sacred songs. The man went away probably more than satisfied with the reward he received. The result was that we had to take stern measures of self-defence,—such an insistent army of singers invaded us. When they found our house impregnable, the musicians began to waylay us in the streets. And as we went out for our walk in the morning, every now and then would appear a *Tambura*,[1] slung over a shoulder, at

[1] An instrument on which the keynote is strummed to accompany singing.

which we felt like game birds at the sight of the muzzle of the hunter's gun. Indeed, so wary did we become that the twang of the *Tambura*, from a distance, scared us away and utterly failed to bag us.

When evening fell, my father would sit out in the verandah facing the garden. I would then be summoned to sing to him. The moon has risen; its beams, passing though the trees, have fallen on the verandah floor; I am singing in the *Behaga* mode:

O Companion in the darkest passage of life . . .

My father with bowed head and clasped hands is intently listening. I can recall this evening scene even now.

I have told of my father's amusement on hearing from Srikantha Babu of my maiden attempt at a devotional poem. I am reminded how, later, I had my recompense. On the occasion of one of our *Magh* festivals several of the hymns were of my composition. One of them was

"The eye sees thee not, who art the pupil of every eye . . ."

My father was then bed-ridden at Chinsurah. He sent for me and my brother Jyoti. He asked my brother to accompany me on the harmonium and got me to sing all my hymns one after the other,—some of them I had to sing twice over. When I had finished he said:

"If the king of the country had known the language and could appreciate its literature, he would doubtless have rewarded the poet. Since that is not so, I suppose I must do it." With which he handed me a cheque.

My father had brought with him some volumes of the Peter Parley series from which to teach me. He selected the life of Benjamin Franklin to begin with. He thought it would read like a story book and be both entertaining and instructive. But he found out his mistake soon after we began it. Benjamin Franklin was much too business-like a person. The narrowness of his calculated morality disgusted my father. In some cases he would get so impatient at the worldly prudence of Franklin that he could not help using strong words of denunciation. Before this I had nothing to do with Sanskrit beyond getting some rules of grammar by rote. My father started me on the second Sanskrit reader at one bound, leaving me to learn the declensions as we went on. The advance I had made in Bengali [1] stood me in good stead. My father also encouraged me to try Sanskrit composition from the very outset. With the vocabulary acquired from my Sanskrit reader I built up grandiose compound words with a pro-

[1] A large proportion of words in the literary Bengali are derived unchanged from the Sanskrit.

fuse sprinkling of sonorous 'm's and 'n's making altogether a most diabolical medley of the language of the gods. But my father never scoffed at my temerity.

Then there were the readings from Proctor's Popular Astronomy which my father explained to me in easy language and which I then rendered into Bengali.

Among the books which my father had brought for his own use, my attention would be mostly attracted by a ten or twelve volume edition of Gibbon's Rome. They looked remarkably dry. "Being a boy," I thought, "I am helpless and read many books because I have to. But why should a grown up person, who need not read unless he pleases, bother himself so?"

(15) *At the Himalayas*

We stayed about a month in Amritsar, and, towards the middle of April, started for the Dalhousie Hills. The last few days at Amritsar seemed as if they would never pass, the call of the Himalayas was so strong upon me.

The terraced hill sides, as we went up in a *jhampan*, were all aflame with the beauty of the flowering spring crops. Every morning we would make a start after our bread and milk, and before sunset take shelter for the night in the next staging bungalow. My eyes had no rest the livelong day, so great was my fear lest anything should escape them. Wherever, at a turn of the road into a gorge, the great forest trees were found clustering closer, and from underneath their shade a little waterfall trickling out, like a little daughter of the hermitage playing at the feet of hoary sages wrapt in meditation, babbling its way over the black moss-covered rocks, there the *jhampan* bearers would put down their burden, and take a rest. Why, oh why, had we to leave such spots behind, cried my thirsting heart, why could we not stay on there for ever?

This is the great advantage of the first vision: the mind is not then aware that there are many more such to come. When this comes to be known to that calculating organ it promptly tries to make a saving in its expenditure of attention. It is only when it believes something to be rare that the mind ceases to be miserly in assigning values. So in the streets of Calcutta I sometimes imagine myself a foreigner, and only then do I discover how much is to be seen, which is lost so long as its full value in attention is not paid. It is the hunger to really see which drives people to travel to strange places.

My father left his little cash-box in my charge.

He had no reason to imagine that I was the fittest custodian of the considerable sums he kept in it for use on the way. He would certainly have felt safer with it in the hands of Kishori, his attendant. So I can only suppose he wanted to train me to the responsibility. One day as we reached the staging bungalow, I forgot to make it over to him and left it lying on a table. This earned me a reprimand.

Every time we got down at the end of a stage, my father had chairs placed for us outside the bungalow and there we sat. As dusk came on the stars blazed out wonderfully through the clear mountain atmosphere, and my father showed me the constellations or treated me to an astronomical discourse.

The house we had taken at Bakrota was on the highest hill-top. Though it was nearing May it was still bitterly cold there, so much so that on the shady side of the hill the winter frosts had not yet melted.

My father was not at all nervous about allowing me to wander about freely even here. Some way below our house there stretched a spur thickly wooded with Deodars. Into this wilderness I would venture alone with my iron-spiked staff. These lordly forest trees, with their huge shadows, towering there like so many giants—what immense lives had they lived through the centuries! And yet this boy of only the other day was crawling round about their trunks unchallenged. I seemed to feel a presence, the moment I stepped into their shade, as of the solid coolness of some old-world saurian, and the checkered light and shade on the leafy mould seemed like its scales.

My room was at one end of the house. Lying on my bed I could see, through the uncurtained windows, the distant snowy peaks shimmering dimly in the starlight. Sometimes, at what hour I could not make out, I, half awakened, would see my father, wrapped in a red shawl, with a lighted lamp in his hand, softly passing by to the glazed verandah where he sat at his devotions. After one more sleep I would find him at my bed-side, rousing me with a push, before yet the darkness of night had passed. This was my appointed hour for memorising Sanscrit declensions. What an excruciatingly wintry awakening from the caressing warmth of my blankets!

By the time the sun rose, my father, after his prayers, finished with me our morning milk, and then, I standing at his side, he would once more hold communion with God, chanting the Upanishads.

Then we would go out for a walk. But how should I keep pace with him? Many an older person could not! So, after a while, I would give it up and scramble back home through some short cut up the mountain side.

After my father's return I had an hour of English lessons. After ten o'clock came the bath in icy-cold water; it was no use asking the servants to temper it with even a jugful of hot water without my father's permission. To give me courage my father would tell of the unbearably freezing baths he had himself been through in his younger days.

Another penance was the drinking of milk. My father was very fond of milk and could take quantities of it. But whether it was a failure to inherit this capacity, or that the unfavourable environment of which I have told proved the stronger, my appetite for milk was grievously wanting. Unfortunately we used to have our milk together. So I had to throw myself on the mercy of the servants; and to their human kindness (or frailty) I was indebted for my goblet being thenceforth more than half full of foam.

After our midday meal lessons began again. But this was more than flesh and blood could stand. My outraged morning sleep *would* have its revenge and I would be toppling over with uncontrollable drowsiness. Nevertheless, no sooner did my father take pity on my plight and let me off, than my sleepiness was off likewise. Then ho! for the mountains.

Staff in hand I would often wander away from one peak to another, but my father did not object. To the end of his life, I have observed, he never stood in the way of our independence. Many a time have I said or done things repugnant alike to his taste and his judgment; with a word he could have stopped me; but he preferred to wait till the prompting to refrain came from within. A passive acceptance by us of the correct and the proper did not satisfy him; he wanted us to love truth with our whole hearts; he knew that mere acquiescence without love is empty. He also knew that truth, if strayed from, can be found again, but a forced or blind acceptance of it from the outside effectually bars the way in.

In my early youth I had conceived a fancy to journey along the Grand Trunk Road, right up to Peshawar, in a bullock cart. No one else supported the scheme, and doubtless there was much to be urged against it as a practical proposition. But when I discoursed on it to my father he was sure it was a splendid idea—travelling by railroad was not worth the name! With which observation he proceeded to recount to me his own adventurous wanderings on foot and horseback.

The Himalayas

Of any chance of discomfort or peril he had not a word to say.

Another time, when I had just been appointed Secretary of the Adi Brahma Samaj, I went over to my father, at his Park Street residence, and informed him that I did not approve of the practice of only Brahmins conducting divine service to the exclusion of other castes. He unhesitatingly gave me permission to correct this if I could. When I got the authority I found I lacked the power. I was able to discover imperfections but could not create perfection! Where were the men? Where was the strength in me to attract the right man? Had I the means to build in the place of what I might break? Till the right man comes any form is better than none—this, I felt, must have been my father's view of the existing order. But he did not for a moment try to discourage me by pointing out the difficulties.

As he allowed me to wander about the mountains at my will, so in the quest for truth he left me free to select my path. He was not deterred by the danger of my making mistakes, he was not alarmed at the prospect of my encountering sorrow. He held up a standard, not a disciplinary rod.

I would often talk to my father of home. Whenever I got a letter from anyone at home I hastened to show it to him. I verily believe I was thus the means of giving him many a picture he could have got from none else. My father also let me read letters to him from my elder brothers. This was his way of teaching me how I ought to write to him; for he by no means underrated the importance of outward forms and ceremonial.

I am reminded of how in one of my second brother's letters he was complaining in somewhat sanscritised phraseology of being worked to death tied by the neck to his post of duty. My father asked me to explain the sentiment. I did it in my way, but he thought a different explanation would fit better. My overweening conceit made me stick to my guns and argue the point with him at length. Another would have shut me up with a snub, but my father patiently heard me out and took pains to justify his view to me.

My father would sometimes tell me funny stories. He had many an anecdote of the gilded youth of his time. There were some exquisites for whose delicate skins the embroidered borders of even Dacca muslins were too coarse, so that to wear muslins with the border torn off became, for a time, the tip-top thing to do.

I was also highly amused to hear from my father for the first time the story of the milkman who was suspected of watering his milk, and the more men one of his customers detailed to look after his milking the bluer the fluid became, till, at last, when the customer himself interviewed him and asked for an explanation, the milkman avowed that if more superintendents had to be satisfied it would only make the milk fit to breed fish!

After I had thus spent a few months with him my father sent me back home with his attendant Kishori.

PART IV

(16) *My Return*

THE chains of the rigorous regime which had bound me snapped for good when I set out from home. On my return I gained an accession of rights. In my case my very nearness had so long kept me out of mind; now that I had been out of sight I came back into view.

I got a foretaste of appreciation while still on the return journey. Travelling alone as I was, with an attendant, brimming with health and spirits, and conspicuous with my gold-worked cap, all the English people I came across in the train made much of me.

When I arrived it was not merely a home-coming from travel, it was also a return from my exile in the servants' quarters to my proper place in the inner apartments. Whenever the inner household assembled in my mother's room I now occupied a seat of honour. And she who was then the youngest bride of our house lavished on me a wealth of affection and regard.

In infancy the loving care of woman is to be had without the asking, and, being as much a necessity as light and air, is as simply accepted without any conscious response; rather does the growing child often display an eagerness to free itself from the encircling web of woman's solicitude. But the unfortunate creature who is deprived of this in its proper season is beggared indeed. This had been my plight. So after being brought up in the servants' quarters when I suddenly came in for a profusion of womanly affection, I could hardly remain unconscious of it.

In the days when the inner apartments were as yet far away from me, they were the elysium of my imagination. The zenana, which from an outside view is a place of confinement, for me was the abode of all freedom. Neither school nor Pandit were there; nor, it seemed to me, did anybody have to do what they did not want to. Its secluded leisure had something mysterious about it; one played about, or did as one liked and had not to render an account of one's doings. Specially so with my youngest sister, to whom, though she attended Nilkamal Pandit's class with us, it seemed to make no difference in his behaviour whether she did her lessons well or ill. Then again, while, by ten o'clock, we had to hurry through our breakfast and be ready for school, she, with her queue dangling behind, walked unconcernedly away, withinwards, tantalising us to distraction.

And when the new bride, adorned with her necklace of gold, came into our house, the mystery of the inner apartments deepened. She, who came from outside and yet became one of us, who was unknown and yet our own, attracted me strangely —with her I burned to make friends. But if by much contriving I managed to draw near, my youngest sister would hustle me off with: "What d'you boys want here—get away outside." The insult added to the disappointment cut me to the quick. Through the glass doors of their cabinets one could catch glimpses of all manner of curious playthings—creations of porcelain and glass—gorgeous in colouring and ornamentation. We were not deemed worthy even to touch them, much less could we muster up courage to ask for any to play with. Nevertheless these rare and wonderful objects, as they were to us boys, served to tinge with an additional attraction the lure of the inner apartments.

Thus had I been kept at arm's length with repeated rebuffs. As the outer world, so, for me, the interior, was unattainable. Wherefore the impressions of it that I did get appeared to me like pictures.

After nine in the evening, my lessons with Aghore Babu over, I am retiring within for the night. A murky flickering lantern is hanging in the long venetian-screened corridor leading from the outer to the inner apartments. At its end this passage turns into a flight of four or five steps, to which the light does not reach, and down which I pass into the galleries running round the first inner quadrangle. A shaft of moonlight slants from the eastern sky into the western angle of these verandahs, leaving the rest in darkness. In this patch of light the maids have gathered and are squatting close together, with legs outstretched, rolling cotton waste into lamp-wicks, and chatting in undertones of their village homes. Many such pictures are indelibly printed on my memory.

Then after our supper, the washing of our hands and feet on the verandah before stretching ourselves on the ample expanse of our bed; whereupon one of the nurses Tinkari or Sankari comes and sits by our heads and softly croons to us the story of the prince travelling on and on over the lonely moor, and, as it comes to an end, silence falls on the room. With my face to the wall I gaze at the black and white patches, made by the plaster of the walls fallen off here and there, showing faintly in the dim light; and out of these I conjure up many a fantastic image as I drop off to sleep. And sometimes, in the middle of the night, I hear through my half-broken sleep the shouts of old Swarup, the watchman, going his rounds from verandah to verandah.

Then came the new order, when I got in profusion from this inner unknown dreamland of my fancies the recognition for which I had all along been pining; when that which naturally should have come day by day was suddenly made good to me with accumulated arrears. I cannot say that my head was not turned.

The little traveller was full of the story of his travels, and, with the strain of each repetition, the narrative got looser and looser till it utterly refused to fit into the facts. Like everything else, alas, a story also gets stale and the glory of the teller suffers likewise; that is why he has to add fresh colouring every time to keep up its freshness.

After my return from the hills I was the principal speaker at my mother's open air gatherings on the roof terrace in the evenings. The temptation to become famous in the eyes of one's mother is as difficult to resist as such fame is easy to earn. While I was at the Normal School, when I first came across the information in some reader that the Sun was hundreds and thousands of times as big as the Earth, I at once disclosed it to my mother. It served to prove that he who was small to look at might yet have a considerable amount of bigness about him. I used also to recite to her the scraps of poetry used as illustrations in the chapter on prosody or rhetoric of our Bengali grammar. Now I retailed at her evening gatherings the astronomical tit-bits I had gleaned from Proctor.

My father's follower Kishori belonged at one time to a band of reciters of Dasarathi's jingling versions of the Epics. While we were together in the hills he often said to me: "Oh, my little brother,[1] if I only had had you in our troupe we could have got up a splendid performance." This would open up to me a tempting picture of wandering as a minstrel boy from place to place, reciting and singing. I learnt from him many of the songs in his repertoire and these were in even greater request than my talks about the photosphere of the Sun or the many moons of Saturn.

But the achievement of mine which appealed most to my mother was that while the rest of the inmates of the inner apartments had to be content with Krittivasa's Bengali rendering of the Ramayana, I had been reading with my father the original of Maharshi Valmiki himself, Sanscrit metre and all. "Read me some of that Ramayana, *do!*" she said, overjoyed at this news which I had given her.

Alas, my reading of Valmiki had been limited to the short extract from his Ramayana given in my Sanskrit reader, and even that I had not fully

[1] Servants call the master and mistress father, and mother, and the children brothers and sisters.

The Servant-maids in the Verandah

mastered. Moreover, on looking over it now, I found that my memory had played me false and much of what I thought I knew had become hazy. But I lacked the courage to plead "I have forgotten" to the eager mother awaiting the display of her son's marvellous talents; so that, in the reading I gave, a large divergence occurred between Valmiki's intention and my explanation. That tender-hearted sage, from his seat in heaven, must have forgiven the temerity of the boy seeking the glory of his mother's approbation, but not so Madhusudan,[1] the taker down of Pride.

My mother, unable to contain her feelings at my extraordinary exploit, wanted all to share her admiration. "You must read this to Dwijendra," (my eldest brother), she said.

"In for it!" thought I, as I put forth all the excuses I could think of, but my mother would have none of them. She sent for my brother Dwijendra, and, as soon as he arrived, greeted him, with: "Just hear Rabi read Valmiki's Ramayan, how splendidly he does it."

It had to be done! But Madhusudan relented and let me off with just a taste of his pride-reducing power. My brother must have been called away while busy with some literary work of his own.

[1] Name of Vishnu in his aspect of slayer of the proud demon, Madhu.

He showed no anxiety to hear me render the Sanscrit into Bengali, and as soon as I had read out a few verses he simply remarked "Very good" and walked away.

After my promotion to the inner apartments I felt it all the more difficult to resume my school life. I resorted to all manner of subterfuges to escape the Bengal Academy. Then they tried putting me at St. Xavier's. But the result was no better.

My elder brothers, after a few spasmodic efforts, gave up all hopes of me—they even ceased to scold me. One day my eldest sister said: "We had all hoped Rabi would grow up to be a man, but he has disappointed us the worst." I felt that my value in the social world was distinctly depreciating; nevertheless I could not make up my mind to be tied to the eternal grind of the school mill which, divorced as it was from all life and beauty, seemed such a hideously cruel combination of hospital and gaol.

One precious memory of St. Xavier's I still hold fresh and pure—the memory of its teachers. Not that they were all of the same excellence. In particular, in those who taught in our class I could discern no reverential resignation of spirit. They were in nowise above the teaching-machine variety of school masters. As it is, the educational engine is remorselessly powerful; when to it is coupled the stone mill of the outward forms of religion the heart of youth is crushed dry indeed. This power-propelled grindstone type we had at St. Xavier's. Yet, as I say, I possess a memory which elevates my impression of the teachers there to an ideal plane.

This is the memory of Father DePeneranda. He had very little to do with us—if I remember right he had only for a while taken the place of one of the masters of our class. He was a Spaniard and seemed to have an impediment in speaking English. It was perhaps for this reason that the boys paid but little heed to what he was saying. It seemed to me that this inattentiveness of his pupils hurt him, but he bore it meekly day after day. I know not why, but my heart went out to him in sympathy. His features were not handsome, but his countenance had for me a strange attraction. Whenever I looked on him his spirit seemed to be in prayer, a deep peace to pervade him within and without.

We had half-an-hour for writing our copybooks; that was a time when, pen in hand, I used to become absent-minded and my thoughts wandered hither and thither. One day Father DePeneranda was in charge of this class. He was pacing up and down behind our benches. He must have noticed more than once that my pen was not moving.

All of a sudden he stopped behind my seat. Bending over me he gently laid his hand on my shoulder and tenderly inquired: "Are you not well, Tagore?" It was only a simple question, but one I have never been able to forget.

I cannot speak for the other boys but I felt in him the presence of a great soul, and even to-day the recollection of it seems to give me a passport into the silent seclusion of the temple of God.

There was another old Father whom all the boys loved. This was Father Henry. He taught in the higher classes; so I did not know him well. But one thing about him I remember. He knew Bengali. He once asked Nirada, a boy in his class, the derivation of his name. Poor Nirada [1] had so long been supremely easy in mind about himself—the derivation of his name, in particular, had never troubled him in the least; so that he was utterly unprepared to answer this question. And yet, with so many abstruse and unknown words in the dictionary, to be worsted by one's own name would have been as ridiculous a mishap as getting run over by one's own carriage, so Nirada unblushingly replied: "*Ni*—privative, *rode*—sun-rays; thence Nirode—that which causes an absence of the sun's rays!"

[1] Nirada is a Sanscrit word meaning *cloud*, being a compound of *nira* = water and *da* = giver. In Bengali it is pronounced *nirode*.

(17) *Home Studies*

Gyan Babu, son of Pandit Vedantavagish, was now our tutor at home. When he found he could not secure my attention for the school course, he gave up the attempt as hopeless and went on a different tack. He took me through Kalidas's "Birth of the War-god," translating it to me as we went on. He also read Macbeth to me, first explaining the text in Bengali, and then confining me to the school room till I had rendered the day's reading into Bengali verse. In this way he got me to translate the whole play. I was fortunate enough to lose this translation and so am relieved to that extent of the burden of my *karma*.

It was Pandit Ramsarvaswa's duty to see to the progress of our Sanskrit. He likewise gave up the fruitless task of teaching grammar to his unwilling pupil, and read Sakuntala with me instead. One day he took it into his head to show my translation of Macbeth to Pandit Vidyasagar and took me over to his house.

Rajkrishna Mukherji had called at the time and was seated with him. My heart went pit-a-pat as I entered the great Pandit's study, packed full of books; nor did his austere visage assist in reviving my courage. Nevertheless, as this was the first time I had had such a distinguished audience, my desire to win renown was strong within me. I returned home, I believe, with some reason for an access of enthusiasm. As for Rajkrishna Babu, he contented himself with admonishing me to be careful to keep the language and metre of the Witches' parts different from that of the human characters.

During my boyhood Bengali literature was meagre in body, and I think I must have finished all the readable and unreadable books that there were at the time. Juvenile literature in those days had not evolved a distinct type of its own—but that I am sure did me no harm. The watery stuff into which literary nectar is now diluted for being served up to the young takes full account of their childishness, but none of them as growing human beings. Children's books should be such as can partly be understood by them and partly not. In our childhood we read every available book from one end to the other; and both what we understood, and what we did not, went on working within us. That is how the world itself reacts on the child consciousness. The child makes its own what it understands, while that which is beyond leads it on a step forward.

When Dinabandhu Mitra's satires came out I

was not of an age for which they were suitable. A kinswoman of ours was reading a copy, but no entreaties of mine could induce her to lend it to me. She used to keep it under lock and key. Its inaccessibility made me want it all the more and I threw out the challenge that read the book I must and would.

One afternoon she was playing cards, and her keys, tied to a corner of her *sari*, hung over her shoulder. I had never paid any attention to cards, in fact I could not stand card games. But my behaviour that day would hardly have borne this out, so engrossed was I in their playing. At last, in the excitement of one side being about to make a score, I seized my opportunity and set about untying the knot which held the keys. I was not skilful, and moreover excited and hasty and so got caught. The owner of the *sari* and of the keys took the fold off her shoulder with a smile, and laid the keys on her lap as she went on with the game.

Then I hit on a stratagem. My kinswoman was fond of *pan*,[1] and I hastened to place some before her. This entailed her rising later on to get rid of the chewed *pan*, and, as she did so, her keys fell off her lap and were replaced over her shoulder. This time they got stolen, the culprit

[1] Betel-leaf and spices.

got off, and the book got read! Its owner tried to scold me, but the attempt was not a success, we both laughed so.

Dr. Rajendralal Mitra used to edit an illustrated monthly miscellany. My third brother had a bound annual volume of it in his bookcase. This I managed to secure and the delight of reading it through, over and over again, still comes back to me. Many a holiday noontide has passed with me stretched on my back on my bed, that square volume on my breast, reading about the Narwhal whale, or the curiosities of justice as administered by the Kazis of old, or the romantic story of Krishna-kumari.

Why do we not have such magazines now-a-days? We have philosophical and scientific articles on the one hand, and insipid stories and travels on the other, but no such unpretentious miscellanies which the ordinary person can read in comfort—such as Chambers's or Cassell's or the Strand in England—which supply the general reader with a simple, but satisfying fare and are of the greatest use to the greatest number.

I came across another little periodical in my young days called the *Abodhabandhu* (ignorant man's friend). I found a collection of its monthly numbers in my eldest brother's library and devoured them day after day, seated on the doorsill of his study, facing a bit of terrace to the South. It was in the pages of this magazine that I made my first acquaintance with the poetry of Viharilal Chakravarti. His poems appealed to me the most of all that I read at the time. The artless flute-strains of his lyrics awoke within me the music of fields and forest-glades.

Into these same pages I have wept many a tear over a pathetic translation of Paul and Virginie. That wonderful sea, the breeze-stirred cocoanut forests on its shore, and the slopes beyond lively with the gambols of mountain goats,—a delightfully refreshing mirage they conjured up on that terraced roof in Calcutta. And oh! the romantic courting that went on in the forest paths of that secluded island, between the Bengali boy reader and little Virginie with the many-coloured kerchief round her head!

Then came Bankim's *Bangadarsan*, taking the Bengali heart by storm. It was bad enough to have to wait till the next monthly number was out, but to be kept waiting further till my elders had done with it was simply intolerable! Now he who will may swallow at a mouthful the whole of *Chandrashekhar* or *Bishabriksha* but the process of longing and anticipating, month after month; of spreading over the long intervals the concentrated joy of each short reading, revolving every instalment over and over in the mind while watching and waiting for the next; the combination of satisfaction with unsatisfied craving, of burning curiosity with its appeasement; these long drawn out delights of going through the original serial none will ever taste again.

The compilations from the old poets by Sarada Mitter and Akshay Sarkar were also of great interest to me. Our elders were subscribers, but not very regular readers, of these series, so that it was not difficult for me to get at them. Vidyapati's quaint and corrupt Maithili language attracted me all the more because of its unintelligibility. I tried to make out his sense without the help of the compiler's notes, jotting down in my own note book all the more obscure words with their context as many times as they occurred. I also noted grammatical peculiarities according to my lights.

(18) *My Home Environment*

One great advantage which I enjoyed in my younger days was the literary and artistic atmosphere which pervaded our house. I remember how, when I was quite a child, I would be leaning against the verandah railings which overlooked the detached building comprising the reception rooms. These rooms would be lighted up every evening. Splendid carriages would draw up under the portico, and visitors would be constantly coming and going. What was happening I could not very well make out, but would keep staring at the rows of lighted casements from my place in the darkness. The intervening space was not great but the gulf between my infant world and these lights was immense.

My elder cousin Ganendra had just got a drama written by Pandit Tarkaratna and was having it staged in the house. His enthusiasm for literature and the fine arts knew no bounds. He was the centre of the group who seem to have been almost consciously striving to bring about from every side the renascence which we see to-day. A pronounced nationalism in dress, literature, music, art and the drama had awakened in and around him. He was a keen student of the history of different countries and had begun but could not complete a historical work in Bengali. He had translated and published the Sanskrit drama, Vikramorvasi, and many a well-known hymn is his composition. He may be said to have given us the lead in writing patriotic poems and songs. This was in the days when the Hindu Mela was an annual institution and there his song "Ashamed am I to sing of India's glories" used to be sung.

I was still a child when my cousin Ganendra died in the prime of his youth, but for those who have once beheld him it is impossible to forget his handsome, tall and stately figure. He had an irresistible social influence. He could draw men round him and keep them bound to him; while his powerful attraction was there, disruption was out of the question. He was one of those—a type peculiar to our country—who, by their personal magnetism, easily establish themselves in the centre of their family or village. In any other country, where large political, social or commercial groups are being formed, such would as naturally become national leaders. The power of organising a large number of men into a corporate group depends on a special kind of genius. Such genius in our country runs to waste, a waste, as pitiful, it seems to me, as that of pulling down a star from the firmament for use as a lucifer match.

I remember still better his younger brother, my cousin Gunendra.[1] He likewise kept the house filled with his personality. His large, gracious heart embraced alike relatives, friends, guests and dependants. Whether in his broad south

[1] Father of the well-known artists Gaganendra and Abanindra. *Ed.*

verandah, or on the lawn by the fountain, or at the tank-edge on the fishing platform, he presided over self-invited gatherings, like hospitality incarnate. His wide appreciation of art and talent kept him constantly radiant with enthusiasm. New ideas of festivity or frolic, theatricals or other entertainments, found in him a ready patron, and with his help would flourish and find fruition.

We were too young then to take any part in these doings, but the waves of merriment and life to which they gave rise came and beat at the doors of our curiosity. I remember how a burlesque composed by my eldest brother was once being rehearsed in my cousin's big drawing room. From our place against the verandah railings of our house we could hear, through the open windows opposite, roars of laughter mixed with the strains of a comic song, and would also occasionally catch glimpses of Akshay Mazumdar's extraordinary antics. We could not gather exactly what the song was about, but lived in hopes of being able to find that out sometime.

I recall how a trifling circumstance earned for me the special regard of cousin Gunendra. Never had I got a prize at school except once for good conduct. Of the three of us my nephew Satya was the best at his lessons. He once did well at some examination and was awarded a prize. As we came home I jumped off the carriage to give the great news to my cousin who was in the garden. "Satya has got a prize" I shouted as I ran to him. He drew me to his knees with a smile. "And have *you* not got a prize?" he asked. "No," said I, "not I, it's Satya." My genuine pleasure at Satya's success seemed to touch my cousin particularly. He turned to his friends and remarked on it as a very creditable trait. I well remember how mystified I felt at this, for I had not thought of my feeling in that light. This prize that I got for not getting a prize did not do me good. There is no harm in making gifts to children, but they should not be rewards. It is not healthy for youngsters to be made self-conscious.

After the mid-day meal cousin Gunendra would attend the estate offices in our part of the house. The office room of our elders was a sort of club where laughter and conversation were freely mixed with matters of business. My cousin would recline on a couch, and I would seize some opportunity of edging up to him.

He usually told me stories from Indian History. I still remember the surprise with which I heard how Clive, after establishing British rule in India, went back home and cut his own throat. On the

My Eldest Brother

one hand new history being made, on the other a tragic chapter hidden away in the mysterious darkness of a human heart. How could there be such dismal failure within and such brilliant success outside? This weighed heavily on my mind the whole day.

Some days cousin Gunendra would not be allowed to remain in any doubt as to the contents of my pocket. At the least encouragement out would come my manuscript book, unabashed. I need hardly state that my cousin was not a severe critic; in point of fact the opinions he expressed would have done splendidly as advertisements. None the less, when in any of my poetry my childishness became too obtrusive, he could not restrain his hearty "Ha! Ha!"

One day it was a poem on "Mother India" and as at the end of one line the only rhyme I could think of meant a cart, I had to drag in that cart in spite of there not being the vestige of a road by which it could reasonably arrive,—the insistent claims of rhyme would not hear of any excuses mere reason had to offer. The storm of laughter with which cousin Gunendra greeted it blew away the cart back over the same impossible path it had come by, and it has not been heard of since.

My eldest brother was then busy with his masterpiece "The Dream Journey," his cushion seat placed in the south verandah, a low desk before him. Cousin Gunendra would come and sit there for a time every morning. His immense capacity for enjoyment, like the breezes of spring, helped poetry to sprout. My eldest brother would go on alternately writing and reading out what he had written, his boisterous mirth at his own conceits making the verandah tremble. My brother wrote a great deal more than he finally used in his finished work, so fertile was his poetic inspiration. Like the superabounding mango flowerets which carpet the shade of the mango topes in spring time, the rejected pages of his "Dream Journey" were to be found scattered all over the house. Had anyone preserved them they would have been to-day a basketful of flowers adorning our Bengali literature.

Eavesdropping at doors and peeping round corners, we used to get our full share of this feast of poetry, so plentiful was it, with so much to spare. My eldest brother was then at the height of his wonderful powers; and from his pen surged, in untiring wave after wave, a tidal flood of poetic fancy, rhyme and expression, filling and overflowing its banks with an exuberantly joyful pæan of triumph. Did we quite understand "The Dream Journey"? But then did we need absolutely to understand in order to enjoy it? We might not have got at the wealth in the ocean depths—what could we have done with it if we had?—but we revelled in the delights of the waves on the shore; and how gaily, at their buffettings, did our life-blood course through every vein and artery!

The more I think of that period the more I realise that we have no longer the thing called a *mujlis*.[1] In our boyhood we beheld the dying rays of that intimate sociability which was characteristic of the last generation. Neighbourly feelings were then so strong that the *mujlis* was a necessity, and those who could contribute to its amenities were in great request. People now-a-days call on each other on business, or as a matter of social duty, but not to foregather by way of *mujlis*. They have not the time, nor are there the same intimate relations! What goings and comings we used to see, how merry were the rooms and verandahs with the hum of conversation and the snatches of laughter! The faculty our predecessors had of becoming the centre of groups and gatherings, of starting and keeping up animated and amusing gossip, has vanished. Men still come and go, but those same verandahs and rooms seem empty and deserted.

[1] In Bengali this word has come to mean an informal uninvited gathering.

In those days everything from furniture to festivity was designed to be enjoyed by the many, so that whatever of pomp or magnificence there might have been did not savour of hauteur. These appendages have since increased in quantity, but they have become unfeeling, and know not the art of making high and low alike feel at home. The bare-bodied, the indigently clad, no longer have the right to use and occupy them, without a permit, on the strength of their smiling faces alone. Those whom we now-a-days seek to imitate in our house-building and furnishing, they have their own society, with its wide hospitality. The mischief with us is that we have lost what we had, but have not the means of building up afresh on the European standard, with the result that our home-life has become joyless. We still meet for business or political purposes, but never for the pleasure of simply meeting one another. We have ceased to contrive opportunities to bring men together simply because we love our fellow-men. I can imagine nothing more ugly than this social miserliness; and, when I look back on those whose ringing laughter, coming straight from their hearts, used to lighten for us the burden of household cares, they seem to have been visitors from some other world.

(19) *Literary Companions*

There came to me in my boyhood a friend whose help in my literary progress was invaluable. Akshay Chowdhury was a school-fellow of my fourth brother. He was an M. A. in English Literature for which his love was as great as his proficiency therein. On the other hand he had an equal fondness for our older Bengali authors and Vaishnava Poets. He knew hundreds of Bengali songs of unknown authorship, and on these he would launch, with voice uplifted, regardless of tune, or consequence, or of the express disapproval of his hearers. Nor could anything, within him or without, prevent his loudly beating time to his own music, for which the nearest table or book served his nimble fingers to rap a vigorous tattoo on, to help to enliven the audience.

He was also one of those with an inordinate capacity for extracting enjoyment from all and sundry. He was as ready to absorb every bit of goodness in a thing as he was lavish in singing its praises. He had an extraordinary gift as a lightning composer of lyrics and songs of no mean merit, but in which he himself had no pride of authorship. He took no further notice of the heaps of scattered scraps of paper on which his pencil writings had been indited. He was as indifferent to his powers as they were prolific.

One of his longer poetic pieces was much appreciated when it appeared in the *Bangadarsan*, and I have heard his songs sung by many who knew nothing at all about their composer.

A genuine delight in literature is much rarer than erudition, and it was this enthusiastic enjoyment in Akshay Babu which used to awaken my own literary appreciation. He was as liberal in his friendships as in his literary criticisms. Among strangers he was as a fish out of water, but among friends discrepancies in wisdom or age made no difference to him. With us boys he was a boy. When he took his leave, late in the evening, from the *mujlis* of our elders, I would buttonhole and drag him to our school room. There, with undiminished geniality he would make himself the life and soul of our little gathering, seated on the top of our study table. On many such occasions I have listened to him going into a rapturous dissertation on some English poem; engaged him in some appreciative discussion, critical inquiry, or hot dispute; or read to him some of my own writings and been rewarded in return with praise unsparing.

My fourth brother Jyotirindra was one of the chief helpers in my literary and emotional training.

He was an enthusiast himself and loved to evoke enthusiasm in others. He did not allow the difference between our ages to be any bar to my free intellectual and sentimental intercourse with him. This great boon of freedom which he allowed me, none else would have dared to do; many even blamed him for it. His companionship made it possible for me to shake off my shrinking sensitiveness. It was as necessary for my soul after its rigorous repression during my infancy as are the monsoon clouds after a fiery summer.

But for such snapping of my shackles I might have become crippled for life. Those in authority are never tired of holding forth the possibility of the abuse of freedom as a reason for withholding it, but without that possibility freedom would not be really free. And the only way of learning how to use properly a thing is through its misuse. For myself, at least, I can truly say that what little mischief resulted from my freedom always led the way to the means of curing mischief. I have never been able to make my own anything which they tried to compel me to swallow by getting hold of me, physically or mentally, by the ears. Nothing but sorrow have I ever gained except when left freely to myself.

My brother Jyotirindra unreservedly let me go my own way to self-knowledge, and only since then could my nature prepare to put forth its thorns, it may be, but likewise its flowers. This experience of mine has led me to dread, not so much evil itself, as tyrannical attempts to create goodness. Of punitive police, political or moral, I have a wholesome horror. The state of slavery which is thus brought on is the worst form of cancer to which humanity is subject.

My brother at one time would spend days at his piano engrossed in the creation of new tunes. Showers of melody would stream from under his dancing fingers, while Akshay Babu and I, seated on either side, would be busy fitting words to the tunes as they grew into shape to help to hold them in our memories.[1] This is how I served my apprenticeship in the composition of songs.

While we were growing to boyhood music was largely cultivated in our family. This had the advantage of making it possible for me to imbibe it, without an effort, into my whole being. It had also the disadvantage of not giving me that technical mastery which the effort of learning step by step alone can give. Of what may be called proficiency in music, therefore, I acquired none.

[1] Systems of notation were not then in use. One of the most popular of the present-day systems was subsequently devised by the writer's brother here mentioned. *Tr.*

Ever since my return from the Himalayas it was a case of my getting more freedom, more and more. The rule of the servants came to an end; I saw to it with many a device that the bonds of my school life were also loosened; nor to my home tutors did I give much scope. Gyan Babu, after taking me through "The Birth of the War-god" and one or two other books in a desultory fashion, went off to take up a legal career. Then came Braja Babu. The first day he put me on to translate "The Vicar of Wakefield." I found that I did not dislike the book; but when this encouraged him to make more elaborate arrangements for the advancement of my learning I made myself altogether scarce.

As I have said, my elders gave me up. Neither I nor they were troubled with any more hopes of my future. So I felt free to devote myself to filling up my manuscript book. And the writings which thus filled it were no better than could have been expected. My mind had nothing in it but hot vapour, and vapour-filled bubbles frothed and eddied round a vortex of lazy fancy, aimless and unmeaning. No forms were evolved, there was only the distraction of movement, a bubbling up, a bursting back into froth. What little of matter there was in it was not mine, but borrowed from other poets. What was my own was the restlessness, the seething tension within me. When motion has been born, while yet the balance of forces has not matured, then is there blind chaos indeed.

My sister-in-law [1] was a great lover of literature. She did not read simply to kill time, but the Bengali books which she read filled her whole mind. I was a partner in her literary enterprises. She was a devoted admirer of "The Dream Journey." So was I; the more particularly as, having been brought up in the atmosphere of its creation, its beauties had become intertwined with every fibre of my heart. Fortunately it was entirely beyond my power of imitation, so it never occurred to me to attempt anything like it.

"The Dream Journey" may be likened to a superb palace of Allegory, with innumerable halls, chambers, passages, corners and niches full of statuary and pictures, of wonderful design and workmanship; and in the grounds around gardens, bowers, fountains and shady nooks in profusion. Not only do poetic thought and fancy abound, but the richness and variety of language and expression is also marvellous. It is not a small thing, this creative power which can bring into being so magnificent a structure complete in all its artistic

[1] The new bride of the house, wife of the writer's fourth brother, above-mentioned. *Tr.*

detail, and that is perhaps why the idea of attempting an imitation never occurred to me.

At this time Viharilal Chakravarti's series of songs called *Sarada Mangal* were coming out in the *Arya Darsan.* My sister-in-law was greatly taken with the sweetness of these lyrics. Most of them she knew by heart. She used often to invite the poet to our house and had embroidered for him a cushion-seat with her own hands. This gave me the opportunity of making friends with him. He came to have a great affection for me, and I took to dropping in at his house at all times of the day, morning, noon or evening. His heart was as large as his body, and a halo of fancy used to surround him like a poetic astral body which seemed to be his truer image. He was always full of true artistic joy, and whenever I have been to him I have breathed in my share of it. Often have I come upon him in his little room on the third storey, in the heat of noonday, sprawling on the cool polished cement floor, writing his poems. Mere boy though I was, his welcome was always so genuine and hearty that I never felt the least awkwardness in approaching him. Then, wrapt in his inspiration and forgetful of all surroundings, he would read out his poems or sing his songs to me. Not that he had much of the gift of song in his voice; but then he was not altogether tuneless, and one could get a fair idea of the intended melody.[1] When with eyes closed he raised his rich deep voice, its expressiveness made up for what it lacked in execution. I still seem to hear some of his songs as he sang them. I would also sometimes set his words to music and sing them to him.

He was a great admirer of Valmiki and Kalidas. I remember how once after reciting a description of the Himalayas from Kalidas with the full strength of his voice, he said: "The succession of long ā sounds here is not an accident. The poet has deliberately repeated this sound all the way from *Devatatma* down to *Nagadhiraja* as an assistance in realising the glorious expanse of the Himalayas."

At the time the height of my ambition was to become a poet like Vihari Babu. I might have even succeeded in working myself up to the belief that I was actually writing like him, but for my sister-in-law, his zealous devotee, who stood in the way. She would keep reminding me of a Sanskrit saying that the unworthy aspirant after poetic fame departs in jeers! Very possibly she knew that if my vanity was once allowed to get the upper hand it would be difficult afterwards to bring it

[1] It may be helpful to the foreign reader to explain that the expert singer of Indian music improvises more or less on the tune outline made over to him by the original composer, so that the latter need not necessarily do more than give a correct idea of such outline. *Tr.*

under control. So neither my poetic abilities nor my powers of song readily received any praise from her; rather would she never let slip an opportunity of praising somebody else's singing at my expense; with the result that I gradually became quite convinced of the defects of my voice. Misgivings about my poetic powers also assailed me; but, as this was the only field of activity left in which I had any chance of retaining my self-respect, I could not allow the judgment of another to deprive me of all hope; moreover, so insistent was the spur within me that to stop my poetic adventure was a matter of sheer impossibility.

(20) *Publishing*

My writings so far had been confined to the family circle. Then was started the monthly called the *Gyanankur*, Sprouting Knowledge, and, as befitted its name it secured an embryo poet as one of its contributors. It began to publish all my poetic ravings indiscriminately, and to this day I have, in a corner of my mind, the fear that, when the day of judgment comes for me, some enthusiastic literary police-agent will institute a search in the inmost zenana of forgotten literature, regardless of the claims of privacy, and bring these out before the pitiless public gaze.

My first prose writing also saw the light in the pages of the *Gyanankur*. It was a critical essay and had a bit of a history.

A book of poems had been published entitled *Bhubanmohini Pratibha.*[1] Akshay Babu in the *Sadharani* and Bhudeb Babu in the *Education Gazette* hailed this new poet with effusive acclamation. A friend of mine, older than myself, whose friendship dates from then, would come and show me letters he had received signed *Bhubanmohini*. He was one of those whom the book had captivated and used frequently to send reverential offerings of books or cloth[2] to the address of the reputed authoress.

Some of these poems were so wanting in restraint both of thought and language that I could not bear the idea of their being written by a woman. The letters that were shown to me made it still less possible for me to believe in the womanliness of the writer. But my doubts did not shake my friend's devotion and he went on with the worship of his idol.

Then I launched into a criticism of the work of this writer. I let myself go, and eruditely held

[1] This would mean "the genius of Bhubanmohini" if that be taken as the author's name.

[2] Gifts of cloth for use as wearing apparel are customary by way of ceremonial offerings of affection, respect or seasonable greeting.

forth on the distinctive features of lyrics and other short poems, my great advantage being that printed matter is so unblushing, so impassively unbetraying of the writer's real attainments. My friend turned up in a great passion and hurled at me the threat that a B. A. was writing a reply. A B. A.! I was struck speechless. I felt the same as in my younger days when my nephew Satya had shouted for a policeman. I could see the triumphal pillar of argument, erected upon my nice distinctions, crumbling before my eyes at the merciless assaults of authoritative quotations; and the door effectually barred against my ever showing my face to the reading public again. Alas, my critique, under what evil star wert thou born! I spent day after day in the direst suspense. But, like Satya's policeman, the B. A. failed to appear.

(21) *Bhanu Singha*

As I have said I was a keen student of the series of old Vaishnava poems which were being collected and published by Babus Akshay Sarkar and Saroda Mitter. Their language, largely mixed with Maithili, I found difficult to understand; but for that very reason I took all the more pains to get at their meaning. My feeling towards them was that same eager curiosity with which I regarded the ungerminated sprout within the seed, or the undiscovered mystery under the dust covering of the earth. My enthusiasm was kept up with the hope of bringing to light some unknown poetical gems as I went deeper and deeper into the unexplored darkness of this treasure-house.

While I was so engaged, the idea got hold of me of enfolding my own writings in just such a wrapping of mystery. I had heard from Akshay Chowdhury the story of the English boy-poet Chatterton. What his poetry was like I had no idea, nor perhaps had Akshay Babu himself. Had we known, the story might have lost its charm. As it happened the melodramatic element in it fired my imagination; for had not so many been deceived by his successful imitation of the classics? And at last the unfortunate youth had died by his own hand. Leaving aside the suicide part I girded up my loins to emulate young Chatterton's exploits.

One noon the clouds had gathered thickly. Rejoicing in the grateful shade of the cloudy midday rest-hour, I lay prone on the bed in my inner room and wrote on a slate the imitation *Maithili* poem *Gahana kusuma kunja majhe*. I was greatly pleased with it and lost no time in reading it out to the first one I came across; of whose understanding a word of it there happened to be not the slightest danger, and who consequently could not but gravely nod and say, "Good, very good indeed!"

To my friend mentioned a while ago I said one day: "A tattered old manuscript has been discovered while rummaging in the *Adi Brahma Samaj* library and from this I have copied some poems by an old Vaishnava Poet named Bhanu Singha;[1] with which I read some of my imitation poems to him. He was profoundly stirred. "These could not have been written even by *Vidyapati* or *Chandidas!*" he rapturously exclaimed. "I really must have that MS. to make over to Akshay Babu for publication."

Then I showed him my manuscript book and conclusively proved that the poems could not have been written by either *Vidyapati* or *Chandidas* because the author happened to be myself. My friend's face fell as he muttered, "Yes, yes, they're not half bad."

When these Bhanu Singha poems were coming out in the *Bharati*, Dr. Nishikanta Chatterjee was in Germany. He wrote a thesis on the lyric poetry of our country comparing it with that of Europe. Bhanu Singha was given a place of honour as one of the old poets such as no modern writer could

[1] The old Vaishnava poets used to bring their name into the last stanza of the poem, this serving as their signature. Bhanu and Rabi both mean the Sun. *Tr.*

have aspired to. This was the thesis on which Nishikanta Chatterjee got his Ph. D.!

Whoever Bhanu Singha might have been, had his writings fallen into the hands of latter-day me, I swear I would not have been deceived. The language might have passed muster; for that which the old poets wrote in was not their mother tongue, but an artificial language varying in the hands of different poets. But there was nothing artificial about their sentiments. Any attempt to test Bhanu Singha's poetry by its ring would have shown up the base metal. It had none of the ravishing melody of our ancient pipes, but only the tinkle of a modern, foreign barrel organ.

(22) *Patriotism*

From an outside point of view many a foreign custom would appear to have gained entry into our family, but at its heart flames a national pride which has never flickered. The genuine regard which my father had for his country never forsook him through all the revolutionary vicissitudes of his life, and this in his descendants has taken shape as a strong patriotic feeling. Love of country was, however, by no means a characteristic of the times of which I am writing. Our educated men then kept at arms' length both the language and thought of their native land. Nevertheless my elder brothers had always cultivated Bengali literature. When on one occasion some new connection by marriage wrote my father an English letter it was promptly returned to the writer.

The *Hindu Mela* was an annual fair which had been instituted with the assistance of our house. Babu Nabagopal Mitter was appointed its manager. This was perhaps the first attempt at a reverential realisation of India as our motherland. My second brother's popular national anthem "*Bharater Jaya*," was composed, then. The singing of songs glorifying the motherland, the recitation of poems of the love of country, the exhibition of indigenous arts and crafts and the encouragement of national talent and skill were the features of this *Mela*.

On the occasion of Lord Curzon's Delhi durbar I wrote a prose-paper—at the time of Lord Lytton's it was a poem. The British Government of those days feared the Russians it is true, but not the pen of a 14-year old poet. So, though my poem lacked none of the fiery sentiments appropriate to my age, there were no signs of any consternation in the ranks of the authorities from Commander-in-chief down to Commissioner of Police. Nor did any lachrymose letter in the *Times* predict a speedy downfall of the Empire for this apathy of its local guardians. I recited my poem under a tree at the Hindu Mela and one of my hearers was Nabin Sen, the poet. He reminded me of this after I had grown up.

My fourth brother, Jyotirindra, was responsible for a political association of which old Rajnarain Bose was the president. It held its sittings in a tumbledown building in an obscure Calcutta lane. Its proceedings were enshrouded in mystery. This mystery was its only claim to be awe-inspiring, for as a matter of fact there was nothing in our deliberations or doings of which government or people need have been afraid. The rest of our family had no idea where we were spending our afternoons. Our front door would be locked, the meeting room in darkness, the watchword a Vedic *mantra*, our talk in whispers. These alone provided us with enough of a thrill, and we wanted nothing more. Mere child as I was, I also was a member. We surrounded ourselves with such an atmosphere of pure frenzy that we always seemed to be soaring aloft on the wings of our enthusiasm. Of bashfulness, diffidence or fear we had none, our main object being to bask in the heat of our own fervour.

Bravery may sometimes have its drawbacks; but it has always maintained a deep hold on the reverence of mankind. In the literature of all countries we find an unflagging endeavour to keep alive this reverence. So in whatever state a particular set of men in a particular locality may be, they cannot escape the constant impact of these stimulating shocks. We had to be content with responding to such shocks, as best we could, by letting loose our imagination, coming together, talking tall and singing fervently.

There can be no doubt that closing up all outlets and barring all openings to a faculty so deep-seated in the nature of man, and moreover so prized by him, creates an unnatural condition favourable to degenerate activity. It is not enough to keep open only the avenues to clerical employment in any comprehensive scheme of Imperial Government—if no road be left for adventurous daring the soul of man will pine for deliverance, and secret passages still be sought, of which the pathways are tortuous and the end unthinkable. I firmly believe that if in those days Government had paraded a frightfulness born of suspicion, then the comedy which the youthful members of this association had been at might have turned into grim tragedy. The play, however, is over, not a brick of Fort-William is any the worse, and we are now smiling at its memory.

My brother Jyotirindra began to busy himself

with a national costume for all India, and submitted various designs to the association. The *Dhoti* was not deemed business-like; trousers were too foreign; so he hit upon a compromise which considerably detracted from the dhoti while failing to improve the trousers. That is to say, the trousers were decorated with the addition of a false dhoti-fold in front and behind. The fearsome thing that resulted from combining a turban with a *Sola-topee* our most enthusiastic member would not have had the temerity to call ornamental. No person of ordinary courage could have dared it, but my brother unflinchingly wore the complete suit in broad day-light, passing through the house of an afternoon to the carriage waiting outside, indifferent alike to the stare of relation or friend, door-keeper or coachman. There may be many a brave Indian ready to die for his country, but there are but few, I am sure, who even for the good of the nation would face the public streets in such pan-Indian garb.

Every Sunday my brother would get up a *Shikar* party. Many of those who joined in it, uninvited, we did not even know. There was a carpenter, a smith and others from all ranks of society. Bloodshed was the only thing lacking in this *shikar*, at least I cannot recall any. Its other appendages were so abundant and satisfying that we felt the absence of dead or wounded game to be a trifling circumstance of no account. As we were out from early morning, my sister-in-law furnished us with a plentiful supply of *luchis* with appropriate accompaniments; and as these did not depend upon the fortunes of our chase we never had to return empty.

The neighbourhood of Maniktola is not wanting in Villa-gardens. We would turn into any one of these at the end, and high- and low-born alike, seated on the bathing platform of a tank, would fling ourselves on the *luchis* in right good earnest, all that was left of them being the vessels they were brought in.

Braja Babu was one of the most enthusiastic of these blood-thirstless *shikaris*. He was the Superintendent of the Metropolitan Institution and had also been our private tutor for a time. One day he had the happy idea of accosting the *mali* (gardener) of a villa-garden into which we had thus trespassed with: "Hallo, has uncle been here lately!" The *mali* lost no time in saluting him respectfully before he replied: "No, Sir, the master hasn't been lately." "All right, get us some green cocoanuts off the trees." We had a fine drink after our *luchis* that day.

A Zamindar in a small way was among our

party. He owned a villa on the river side. One day we had a picnic there together, in defiance of caste rules. In the afternoon there was a tremendous storm. We stood on the river-side stairs leading into the water and shouted out songs to its accompaniment. I cannot truthfully assert that all the seven notes of the scale could properly be distinguished in Rajnarain Babu's singing, nevertheless he sent forth his voice and, as in the old Sanskrit works the text is drowned by the notes, so in Rajnarain Babu's musical efforts the vigorous play of his limbs and features overwhelmed his feebler vocal performance; his head swung from side to side marking time, while the storm played havoc with his flowing beard. It was late in the night when we turned homewards in a hackney carriage. By that time the storm clouds had dispersed and the stars twinkled forth. The darkness had become intense, the atmosphere silent, the village roads deserted, and the thickets on either side filled with fireflies like a carnival of sparks scattered in some noiseless revelry.

One of the objects of our association was to encourage the manufacture of lucifer matches, and similar small industries. For this purpose each member had to contribute a tenth of his income. Matches had to be made, but matchwood was difficult to get; for though we all know with what fiery energy a bundle of *khangras*[1] can be wielded in capable hands, the thing that burns at its touch is not a lamp wick. After many experiments we succeeded in making a boxful of matches. The patriotic enthusiasm which was thus evidenced did not constitute their only value, for the money that was spent in their making might have served to light the family hearth for the space of a year. Another little defect was that these matches could not be got to burn unless there was a light handy to touch them up with. If they could only have inherited some of the patriotic flame of which they were born they might have been marketable even to-day.

News came to us that some young student was trying to make a power loom. Off we went to see it. None of us had the knowledge with which to test its practical usefulness, but in our capacity for believing and hoping we were inferior to none. The poor fellow had got into a bit of debt over the cost of his machine which we repaid for him. Then one day we found Braja Babu coming over to our house with a flimsy

[1] The dried and stripped centre-vein of a cocoanut leaf gives a long tapering stick of the average thickness of a match stick, and a bundle of these goes to make the common Bengal household broom which in the hands of the housewife is popularly supposed to be useful in keeping the whole household in order from husband downwards. Its effect on a bare back is here alluded to.—*Tr.*

country towel tied round his head. "Made in our loom!" he shouted as with hands uplifted he executed a war-dance. The outside of Braja Babu's head had then already begun to ripen into grey!

At last some worldly-wise people came and joined our society, made us taste of the fruit of knowledge, and broke up our little paradise.

When I first knew Rajnarain Babu, I was not old enough to appreciate his many-sidedness. In him were combined many opposites. In spite of his hoary hair and beard he was as young as the youngest of us, his venerable exterior serving only as a white mantle for keeping his youth perpetually fresh. Even his extensive learning had not been able to do him any damage, for it left him absolutely simple. To the end of his life the incessant flow of his hearty laughter suffered no check, neither from the gravity of age, nor ill-health, nor domestic affliction, nor profundity of thought, nor variety of knowledge, all of which had been his in ample measure. He had been a favourite pupil of Richardson and brought up in an atmosphere of English learning, nevertheless he flung aside all obstacles due to his early habit and gave himself up lovingly and devotedly to Bengali literature. Though the meekest of men, he was full of fire which flamed its fiercest in his patriotism, as though to burn to ashes the shortcomings and destitution of his country. The memory of this smile-sweetened fervour-illumined lifelong-youthful saint is one that is worth cherishing by our countrymen.

(23) *The Bharati*

On the whole the period of which I am writing was for me one of ecstatic excitement. Many a night have I spent without sleep, not for any particular reason but from a mere desire to do the reverse of the obvious. I would keep up reading in the dim light of our school room all alone; the distant church clock would chime every quarter as if each passing hour was being put up to auction; and the loud *Haribols* of the bearers of the dead, passing along Chitpore Road on their way to the Nimtollah cremation ground, would now and then resound. Through some summer moonlight nights I would be wandering about like an unquiet spirit among the lights and shadows of the tubs and pots on the garden of the roof-terrace.

Those who would dismiss this as sheer poetising would be wrong. The very earth in spite of its having aged considerably surprises us occasionally by its departure from sober stability; in the days of its youth, when it had not become hardened and crusty, it was effusively volcanic and indulged in many a wild escapade. In the days of man's first youth the same sort of thing happens. So long as the materials which go to form his life have not taken on their final shape they are apt to be turbulent in the process of their formation.

This was the time when my brother Jyotirindra decided to start the *Bharati* with our eldest brother as editor, giving us fresh food for enthusiasm. I was then just sixteen, but I was not left out of the editorial staff. A short time before, in all the insolence of my youthful vanity, I had written a criticism of the *Meghanadabadha*. As acidity is characteristic of the unripe mango so is abuse of the immature critic. When other powers are lacking, the power of pricking seems to be at its sharpest. I had thus sought immortality by leaving my scratches on that immortal epic. This impudent criticism was my first contribution to the Bharati.

In the first volume I also published a long poem called *Kavikahini*, The Poet's Story. It was the product of an age when the writer had seen practically nothing of the world except an exaggerated image of his own nebulous self. So the hero of the story was naturally a poet, not the writer as he was, but as he imagined or desired himself to seem. It would hardly be correct to say that he desired to *be* what he portrayed; that represented more what he thought was expected of him, what would make the world admiringly nod and say: "Yes, a poet indeed, quite the correct thing." In it was a great parade of universal love, that pet subject of the budding poet, which sounds as big as it is easy to talk about. While yet any truth has not dawned upon one's own mind, and others' words are one's only stock-in-trade, simplicity and restraint in expression are not possible. Then, in the endeavour to display magnified that which is really big in itself, it becomes impossible to avoid a grotesque and ridiculous exhibition.

When I blush to read these effusions of my boyhood I am also struck with the fear that very possibly in my later writings the same distortion, wrought by straining after effect, lurks in a less obvious form. The loudness of my voice, I doubt not, often drowns the thing I would say; and some day or other Time will find me out.

The *Kavikahini* was the first work of mine to appear in book form. When I went with my second brother to Ahmedabad, some enthusiastic friend of mine took me by surprise by printing and publishing it and sending me a copy. I cannot say that he did well, but the feeling that was roused in me at the time did not resemble that of an indignant judge. He got his punishment, however, not from the author, but from the public who hold the purse strings. I have heard that the dead load of the books lay, for many a long day, heavy on the shelves of the booksellers and the mind of the luckless publisher.

Writings of the age at which I began to contribute to the *Bharati* cannot possibly be fit for publication. There is no better way of ensuring repentance at maturity than to rush into print too early. But it has one redeeming feature: the irresistible impulse to see one's writings in print exhausts itself during early life. Who are the readers, what do they say, what printers' errors have remained uncorrected, these and the like worries run their course as infantile maladies and leave one leisure in later life to attend to one's literary work in a healthier frame of mind.

Bengali literature is not old enough to have elaborated those internal checks which can serve to control its votaries. As experience in writing is gained the Bengali writer has to evolve the restraining force from within himself. This makes it impossible for him to avoid the creation of a great deal of rubbish during a considerable length of time. The ambition to work wonders with the modest gifts at one's disposal is bound to be an obsession in the beginning, so that the effort to transcend at every step one's natural powers, and therewith the bounds of truth and beauty, is always visible in early writings. To recover one's normal self, to learn to respect one's powers as they are, is a matter of time.

However that may be, I have left much of youthful folly to be ashamed of, besmirching the pages of the *Bharati;* and this shames me not for its literary defects alone but for its atrocious impudence, its extravagant excesses and its high-sounding artificiality. At the same time I am free to recognise that the writings of that period were pervaded with an enthusiasm the value of which cannot be small. It was a period to which, if error was natural, so was the boyish faculty of hoping, believing and rejoicing. And if the fuel of error was necessary for feeding the flame of enthusiasm then while that which was fit to be reduced to ashes will have become ash, the good work done by the flame will not have been in vain in my life.

PART V

(24) *Ahmedabad*

WHEN the *Bharati* entered upon its second year, my second brother proposed to take me to England; and when my father gave his consent, this further unasked favour of providence came on me as a surprise.

As a first step I accompanied my brother to Ahmedabad where he was posted as judge. My sister-in-law with her children was then in England, so the house was practically empty.

The Judge's house is known as *Shahibagh* and was a palace of the Badshahs of old. At the foot of the wall supporting a broad terrace flowed the thin summer stream of the Savarmati river along one edge of its ample bed of sand. My brother used to go off to his court, and I would be left all alone in the vast expanse of the palace, with only the cooing of the pigeons to break the midday stillness; and an unaccountable curiosity kept me wandering about the empty rooms.

Into the niches in the wall of a large chamber my brother had put his books. One of these was a gorgeous edition of Tennyson's works, with big print and numerous pictures. The book, for me, was as silent as the palace, and, much in the same way I wandered among its picture plates.

Not that I could not make anything of the text, but it spoke to me more like inarticulate cooings than words. In my brother's library I also found a book of collected Sanskrit poems edited by Dr. Haberlin and printed at the old Serampore press. This was also beyond my understanding but the sonorous Sanskrit words, and the march of the metre, kept me tramping among the *Amaru Shataka* poems to the mellow roll of their drum-call.

In the upper room of the palace tower was my lonely hermit cell, my only companions being a nest of wasps. In the unrelieved darkness of the night I slept there alone. Sometimes a wasp or two would drop off the nest on to my bed, and if perchance I happened to roll on one, the meeting was unpleasing to the wasp and keenly discomforting to me.

On moonlight nights pacing round and round the extensive terrace overlooking the river was one of my caprices. It was while so doing that I first composed my own tunes for my songs. The song addressed to the Rose-maiden was one of these, and it still finds a place in my published works.

Finding how imperfect was my knowledge of English I set to work reading through some English books with the help of a dictionary. From my earliest years it was my habit not to let any want of complete comprehension interfere with my reading on, quite satisfied with the structure which my imagination reared on the bits which I understood here and there. I am reaping even to-day both the good and bad effects of this habit.

(25) *England*

After six months thus spent in Ahmedabad we started for England. In an unlucky moment I began to write letters about my journey to my relatives and to the *Bharati*. Now it is beyond my power to call them back. These were nothing but the outcome of youthful bravado. At that age the mind refuses to admit that its greatest pride is in its power to understand, to accept, to respect; and that modesty is the best means of enlarging its domain. Admiration and praise are looked upon as a sign of weakness or surrender, and the desire to cry down and hurt and demolish with argument gives rise to this kind of intellectual fireworks. These attempts of mine to establish my superiority by revilement might have occasioned me amusement to-day, had not their want of straightness and common courtesy been too painful.

From my earliest years I had had practically no

commerce with the outside world. To be plunged in this state, at the age of 17, into the midst of the social sea of England would have justified considerable misgiving as to my being able to keep afloat. But as my sister-in-law happened to be in Brighton with her children I weathered the first shock of it under her shelter.

Winter was then approaching. One evening as we were chatting round the fireside, the children came running to us with the exciting news that it had been snowing. We at once went out. It was bitingly cold, the sky filled with white moonlight, the earth covered with white snow. It was not the face of Nature familiar to me, but something quite different—like a dream. Everything near seemed to have receded far away, leaving the still white figure of an ascetic steeped in deep meditation. The sudden revelation, on the mere stepping outside a door, of such wonderful, such immense beauty had never before come upon me.

My days passed merrily under the affectionate care of my sister-in-law and in boisterous rompings with the children. They were greatly tickled at my curious English pronunciation, and though in the rest of their games I could whole-heartedly join, this I failed to see the fun of. How could I explain to them that there was no logical means of distinguishing between the sound of *a* in warm and *o* in worm. Unlucky that I was, I had to bear the brunt of the ridicule which was more properly the due of the vagaries of English spelling.

I became quite an adept in inventing new ways of keeping the children occupied and amused. This art has stood me in good stead many a time thereafter, and its usefulness for me is not yet over. But I no longer feel in myself the same unbounded profusion of ready contrivance. That was the first opportunity I had for giving my heart to children, and it had all the freshness and overflowing exuberance of such a first gift.

But I had not set out on this journey to exchange a home beyond the seas for the one on this side. The idea was that I should study Law and come back a barrister. So one day I was put into a public school in Brighton. The first thing the Headmaster said after scanning my features was: "What a splendid head you have!" This detail lingers in my memory because she, who at home was an enthusiast in her self-imposed duty of keeping my vanity in check, had impressed on me that my cranium [1] and features generally, compared with that of many another were barely of a medium order. I hope the reader will not fail to count it to my credit that I implicitly believed her, and inwardly deplored the parsimony

[1] There was a craze for phrenology at the time. *Tr.*

of the Creator in the matter of my making. On many another occasion, finding myself estimated by my English acquaintances differently from what I had been accustomed to be by her, I was led to seriously worry my mind over the divergence in the standard of taste between the two countries!

One thing in the Brighton school seemed very wonderful: the other boys were not at all rude to me. On the contrary they would often thrust oranges and apples into my pockets and run away. I can only ascribe this uncommon behaviour of theirs to my being a foreigner.

I was not long in this school either—but that was no fault of the school. Mr. Tarak Palit[1] was then in England. He could see that this was not the way for me to get on, and prevailed upon my brother to allow him to take me to London, and leave me there to myself in a lodging house. The lodgings selected faced the Regent Gardens. It was then the depth of winter. There was not a leaf on the row of trees in front which stood staring at the sky with their scraggy snow-covered branches—a sight which chilled my very bones.

For the newly arrived stranger there can hardly

[1] Latterly Sir Tarak Palit, a life-long friend of the writer's second brother. *Tr.*

be a more cruel place than London in winter. I knew no one near by, nor could I find my way about. The days of sitting alone at a window, gazing at the outside world, came back into my life. But the scene in this case was not attractive. There was a frown on its countenance; the sky turbid; the light lacking lustre like a dead man's eye; the horizon shrunk upon itself; with never an inviting smile from a broad hospitable world. The room was but scantily furnished, but there happened to be a harmonium which, after the daylight came to its untimely end, I used to play upon according to my fancy. Sometimes Indians would come to see me; and, though my acquaintance with them was but slight, when they rose to leave I felt inclined to hold them back by their coat-tails.

While living in these rooms there was one who came to teach me Latin. His gaunt figure with its worn-out clothing seemed no more able than the naked trees to withstand the winter's grip. I do not know what his age was but he clearly looked older than his years. Some days in the course of our lessons he would suddenly be at a loss for some word and look vacant and ashamed. His people at home counted him a crank. He had become possessed of a theory. He believed that in each age some one dominant idea is manifested in every human society in all parts of the world; and though it may take different shapes under different degrees of civilisation, it is at bottom one and the same; nor is such idea taken from one by another by any process of adoption, for this truth holds good even where there is no intercourse. His great preoccupation was the gathering and recording of facts to prove this theory. And while so engaged his home lacked food, his body clothes. His daughters had but scant respect for his theory and were perhaps constantly upbraiding him for his infatuation. Some days one could see from his face that he had lighted upon some new proof, and that his thesis had correspondingly advanced. On these occasions I would broach the subject, and wax enthusiastic at his enthusiasm. On other days he would be steeped in gloom, as if his burden was too heavy to bear. Then would our lessons halt at every step; his eyes wander away into empty space; and his mind refuse to be dragged into the pages of the first Latin Grammar. I felt keenly for the poor body-starved theory-burdened soul, and though I was under no delusion as to the assistance I got in my Latin, I could not make up my mind to get rid of him. This pretence of learning Latin lasted as long as I was at these lodgings. When on the eve of leaving them I offered to settle his dues he said piteously: "I have done nothing, and only wasted your time, I cannot accept any payment from you." It was with great difficulty that I got him at last to take his fees.

Though my Latin tutor had never ventured to trouble me with the proofs of his theory, yet up to this day I do not disbelieve it. I am convinced that the minds of men are connected through some deep-lying continuous medium, and that a disturbance in one part is by it secretly communicated to others.

Mr. Palit next placed me in the house of a coach named Barker. He used to lodge and prepare students for their examinations. Except his mild little wife there was not a thing with any pretensions to attractiveness about this household. One can understand how such a tutor can get pupils, for these poor creatures do not often get the chance of making a choice. But it is painful to think of the conditions under which such men get wives. Mrs. Barker had attempted to console herself with a pet dog, but when Barker wanted to punish his wife he tortured the dog. So that her affection for the unfortunate animal only made for an enlargement of her field of sensibility.

From these surroundings, when my sister-in-law sent for me to Torquay in Devonshire, I was only too glad to run off to her. I cannot tell how happy I was with the hills there, the sea, the flower-covered meadows, the shade of the pine woods, and my two little restlessly playful companions. I was nevertheless sometimes tormented with questionings as to why, when my eyes were so surfeited with beauty, my mind saturated with joy, and my leisure-filled days crossing over the limitless blue of space freighted with unalloyed happiness, there should be no call of poetry to me. So one day off I went along the rocky shore, armed with MS. book and umbrella, to fulfil my poet's destiny. The spot I selected was of undoubted beauty, for that did not depend on my rhyme or fancy. There was a flat bit of overhanging rock reaching out as with a perpetual eagerness over the waters; rocked on the foam-flecked waves of the liquid blue in front, the sunny sky slept smilingly to its lullaby; behind, the shade of the fringe of pines lay spread like the slipped off garment of some languorous wood nymph. Enthroned on that seat of stone I wrote a poem *Magnatari* (the sunken boat). I might have believed to-day that it was good, had I taken the precaution of sinking it then in the sea. But such consolation is not open to me, for it happens to be existing in the body; and though banished from my published works, a writ might yet cause it to be produced.

The messenger of duty however was not idle. Again came its call and I returned to London. This time I found a refuge in the household of

Dr. Scott. One fine evening with bag and baggage I invaded his home. Only the white haired Doctor, his wife and their eldest daughter were there. The two younger girls, alarmed at this incursion of an Indian stranger had gone off to stay with a relative. I think they came back home only after they got the news of my not being dangerous.

In a very short time I became like one of the family. Mrs. Scott treated me as a son, and the heartfelt kindness I got from her daughters is rare even from one's own relations.

One thing struck me when living in this family—that human nature is everywhere the same. We are fond of saying, and I also believed, that the devotion of an Indian wife to her husband is something unique, and not to be found in Europe. But I at least was unable to discern any difference between Mrs. Scott and an ideal Indian wife. She was entirely wrapped up in her husband. With their modest means there was no fussing about of too many servants, and Mrs. Scott attended to every detail of her husband's wants herself. Before he came back home from his work of an evening, she would arrange his arm-chair and woollen slippers before the fire with her own hands. She would never allow herself to forget for a moment the things he liked, or the behaviour which pleased him. She would go over the house every morning, with their only maid, from attic to kitchen, and the brass rods on the stairs and the door knobs and fittings would be scrubbed and polished till they shone again. Over and above this domestic routine there were the many calls of social duty. After getting through all her daily duties she would join with zest in our evening readings and music, for it is not the least of the duties of a good housewife to make real the gaiety of the leisure hour.

Some evenings I would join the girls in a table-turning seance. We would place our fingers on a small tea table and it would go capering about the room. It got to be so that whatever we touched began to quake and quiver. Mrs. Scott did not quite like all this. She would sometimes gravely shake her head and say she had her doubts about its being right. She bore it bravely, however, not liking to put a damper on our youthful spirits. But one day when we put our hands on Dr. Scott's chimneypot to make it turn, that was too much for her. She rushed up in a great state of mind and forbade us to touch it. She could not bear the idea of Satan having anything to do, even for a moment, with her husband's head-gear.

In all her actions her reverence for her husband was the one thing that stood out. The memory of her sweet self-abnegation makes it clear to me that the ultimate perfection of all womanly love is to be found in reverence; that where no extraneous cause has hampered its true development woman's love naturally grows into worship. Where the appointments of luxury are in profusion, and frivolity tarnishes both day and night, this love is degraded, and woman's nature finds not the joy of its perfection.

I spent some months here. Then it was time for my brother to return home, and my father wrote to me to accompany him. I was delighted at the prospect. The light of my country, the sky of my country, had been silently calling me. When I said good bye Mrs. Scott took me by the hand and wept. "Why did you come to us," she said, "if you must go so soon?" That household no longer exists in London. Some of the members of the Doctor's family have departed to the other world, others are scattered in places unknown to me. But it will always live in my memory.

One winter's day, as I was passing through a street in Tunbridge Wells, I saw a man standing on the road side. His bare toes were showing through his gaping boots, his breast was partly uncovered. He said nothing to me, perhaps because begging was forbidden, but he looked up at my face just for a moment. The coin I gave him was perhaps more valuable than he expected, for, after I had gone on a bit, he came after me and said: "Sir, you have given me a gold piece by mistake," with which he offered to return it to me. I might not have particularly remembered this, but for a similar thing which happened on another occasion. When I first reached the Torquay railway station a porter took my luggage to the cab outside. After searching my purse for small change in vain, I gave him half-a-crown as the cab started. After a while he came running after us, shouting to the cabman to stop. I thought to myself that finding me to be such an innocent he had hit upon some excuse for demanding more. As the cab stopped he said: "You must have mistaken a half-crown piece for a penny, Sir!"

I cannot say that I have never been cheated while in England, but not in any way which it would be fair to hold in remembrance. What grew chiefly upon me, rather, was the conviction that only those who are trustworthy know how to trust. I was an unknown foreigner, and could have easily evaded payment with impunity, yet no London shopkeeper ever mistrusted me.

During the whole period of my stay in England I was mixed up in a farcical comedy which I had to play out from start to finish. I happened to get acquainted with the widow of some departed high Anglo-Indian official. She was good enough to call me by the pet-name Ruby. Some Indian friend of hers had composed a doleful poem in English in memory of her husband. It is needless to expatiate on its poetic merit or felicity of diction. As my ill-luck would have it, the composer had indicated that the dirge was to be chanted to the mode *Behaga*. So the widow one day entreated me to sing it to her thus. Like the silly innocent that I was, I weakly acceded. There was unfortunately no one there but I who could realise the atrociously ludicrous way in which the *Behaga* mode combined with those absurd verses. The widow seemed intensely touched to hear the Indian's lament for her husband sung to its native melody. I thought that there the matter ended, but that was not to be.

I frequently met the widowed lady at different social gatherings, and when after dinner we joined the ladies in the drawing room, she would ask me to sing that *Behaga*. Everyone else would anticipate some extraordinary specimen of Indian music and would add their entreaties to hers. Then from her pocket would come forth printed copies of that fateful composition, and my ears begin to redden and tingle. And at last, with bowed head and quavering voice I would have to make a beginning—but too keenly conscious that to none else in the room but me was this performance sufficiently heartrending. At the end, amidst much suppressed tittering, there would come a chorus of "Thank you very much!" "How interesting!" And in spite of its being winter I would perspire all over. Who would have predicted at my birth or at his death what a severe blow to me would be the demise of this estimable Anglo-Indian!

Then, for a time, while I was living with Dr. Scott and attending lectures at the University College, I lost touch with the widow. She was in a suburban locality some distance away from London, and I frequently got letters from her inviting me there. But my dread of that dirge kept me from accepting these invitations. At length I got a pressing telegram from her. I was on my way to college when this telegram reached me and my stay in England was then about to come to its close. I thought to myself I ought to see the widow once more before my departure, and so yielded to her importunity.

Instead of coming home from college I went straight to the railway station. It was a horrible day, bitterly cold, snowing and foggy. The station I was bound for was the terminus of the line. So I felt quite easy in mind and did not think it worth while to inquire about the time of arrival.

All the station platforms were coming on the right hand side, and in the right hand corner seat I had ensconced myself reading a book. It had already become so dark that nothing was visible outside. One by one the other passengers got down at their destinations. We reached and left the station just before the last one. Then the train stopped again, but there was nobody to be seen, nor any lights or platform. The mere passenger has no means of divining why trains should sometimes stop at the wrong times and places, so, giving up the attempt, I went on with my reading. Then the train began to move backwards. There seems to be no accounting for railway eccentricity, thought I as I once more returned to my book. But when we came right back to the previous station, I could remain indifferent no longer. "When are we getting to———" I inquired at the station. "You are just coming from there," was the reply. "Where are we going now, then?" I asked, thoroughly flurried. "To London." I thereupon understood that this was a shuttle train. On inquiring about the next train to ——— I was informed that there were no more trains that night. And in reply to my next question I gathered that there was no inn within five miles.

I had left home after breakfast at ten in the morning, and had had nothing since. When abstinence is the only choice, an ascetic frame of mind comes easy. I buttoned up my thick overcoat to the neck and seating myself under a platform lamp went on with my reading. The book I had with me was Spencer's *Data of Ethics*, then recently published. I consoled myself with the thought that I might never get another such opportunity of concentrating my whole attention on such a subject.

After a short time a porter came and informed me that a special was running and would be in in half an hour. I felt so cheered up by the news that I could not go on any longer with the *Data of Ethics*. Where I was due at seven I arrived at length at nine. "What is this, Ruby?" asked my hostess. "Whatever have you been doing with yourself?" I was unable to take much pride in the account of my wonderful adventures which I gave her. Dinner was over; nevertheless, as my misfortune was hardly my fault, I did not expect condign punishment, especially as the dispenser was a woman. But all that the widow of the high Anglo-Indian official said to me was: "Come along, Ruby, have a cup of tea."

I never was a tea-drinker, but in the hope that it might be of some assistance in allaying my consuming hunger I managed to swallow a cup of strong decoction with a couple of dry biscuits. When I at length reached the drawing room I found a gathering of elderly ladies and among them one pretty young American who was engaged to a nephew of my hostess and seemed busy going through the usual premarital love passages.

"Let's have some dancing," said my hostess. I was neither in the mood nor bodily condition for that exercise. But it is the docile who achieve the most impossible things in this world; so, though the dance was primarily got up for the benefit of the engaged couple, I had to dance with the ladies of considerably advanced age, with only the tea and biscuits between myself and starvation.

But my sorrows did not end here. "Where are you putting up for the night?" asked my hostess. This was a question for which I was not prepared. While I stared at her, speechless, she explained that as the local inn would close at midnight I had better betake myself thither without further delay. Hospitality, however, was not entirely wanting for I had not to find the inn unaided, a servant showing me the way there with a lantern. At first I thought this might prove a blessing in disguise, and at once proceeded to make inquiries for food: flesh, fish or vegetable, hot or cold, anything! I was told that drinks I could have in any variety but nothing to eat. Then I looked to slumber for forgetfulness, but there seemed to be no room even in her world-embracing lap. The sand-stone floor of the bed-room was icy cold, an old bedstead and worn-out wash-stand being its only furniture.

In the morning the Anglo-Indian widow sent for me to breakfast. I found a cold repast spread out, evidently the remnants of last night's dinner. A small portion of this, lukewarm or cold, offered to me last night could not have hurt anyone, while my dancing might then have been less like the agonised wrigglings of a landed carp.

After breakfast my hostess informed me that the lady for whose delectation I had been invited to sing was ill in bed, and that I would have to serenade her from her bed-room door. I was made to stand up on the staircase landing. Pointing to a closed door the widow said: "That's where she is." And I gave voice to that *Behaga* dirge facing the mysterious unknown on the other side. Of what happened to the invalid as the result I have yet received no news.

After my return to London I had to expiate in bed the consequences of my fatuous complaisance. Dr. Scott's girls implored me, on my conscience, not to take this as a sample of English hospitality. It was the effect of India's salt, they protested.

(26) *Loken Palit*

While I was attending lectures on English literature at the University College, Loken Palit was my class fellow. He was about 4 years younger than I. At the age I am writing these reminiscences a difference of 4 years is not perceptible. But it is difficult for friendship to bridge the gulf between 17 and 13. Lacking the weight of years the boy is always anxious to keep up the dignity of seniority. But this did not raise any barrier in my mind in the case of the boy Loken, for I could not feel that he was in any way my junior.

Boy and girl students sat together in the College library for study. This was the place for our tete-a-tete. Had we been fairly quiet about it none need have complained, but my young friend was so surcharged with high spirits that at the least provocation they would burst forth as laughter. In all countries girls have a perverse degree of application to their studies, and I feel repentant as I recall the multitude of reproachful blue eyes which vainly showered disapprobation on our unrestrained merriment. But in those days I felt not the slightest sympathy with the distress of disturbed studiousness. By the grace of Providence I have never had a headache in my life, nor a moment of compunction for interrupted school studies.

With our laughter as an almost unbroken accompaniment we managed also to do a bit of literary discussion, and, though Loken's reading of Bengali literature was less extensive than mine, he made up for that by the keenness of his intellect. Among the subjects we discussed was Bengali orthography.

The way it arose was this. One of the Scott girls wanted me to teach her Bengali. When taking her through the alphabet I expressed my pride that Bengali spelling has a conscience, and does not delight in overstepping rules at every step. I made clear to her how laughable would have been the waywardness of English spelling but for the tragic compulsion we were under to cram it for our examinations. But my pride had a fall. It transpired that Bengali spelling was quite as impatient of bondage, but that habit had blinded me to its transgressions.

Then I began to search for the laws regulating its lawlessness. I was quite surprised at the wonderful assistance which Loken proved to be in this matter.

After Loken had got into the Indian Civil Service, and returned home, the work, which had in the University College library had its source in rippling merriment, flowed on in a widening stream. Loken's boisterous delight in literature was as the wind in the sails of my literary adventure. And when at the height of my youth I was driving the tandem of prose and poetry at a furious rate, Loken's unstinted appreciation kept my energies from flagging for a moment. Many an extraordinary prose or poetical flight have I taken in his bungalow in the moffussil. On many an occasion did our literary and musical gatherings assemble under the auspices of the evening star to disperse, as did the lamplights at the breezes of dawn, under the morning star.

Of the many lotus flowers at *Saraswati's*[1] feet the blossom of friendship must be her favorite. I have not come across much of golden pollen in her lotus bank, but have nothing to complain of as regards the profusion of the sweet savour of good-fellowship.

(27) *The Broken Heart*

While in England I began another poem, which I went on with during my journey home, and finished after my return. This was published under the name of *Bhagna Hriday*, The Broken

[1] Saraswati, the goddess of learning, is depicted in Bengal as clad in white and seated among a mass of lotus flowers. *Tr.*

Heart. At the time I thought it very good. There was nothing strange in the writer's thinking so; but it did not fail to gain the appreciation of the readers of the time as well. I remember how, after it came out, the chief minister of the late Raja of Tipperah called on me solely to deliver the message that the Raja admired the poem and entertained high hopes of the writer's future literary career.

About this poem of my eighteenth year let me set down here what I wrote in a letter when I was thirty:

> When I began to write the *Bhagna Hriday* I was eighteen—neither in my childhood nor my youth. This borderland age is not illumined with the direct rays of Truth;—its reflection is seen here and there, and the rest is shadow. And like twilight shades its imaginings are long-drawn and vague, making the real world seem like a world of phantasy. The curious part of it is that not only was I eighteen, but everyone around me seemed to be eighteen likewise; and we all flitted about in the same baseless, substanceless world of imagination, where even the most intense joys and sorrows seemed like the joys and sorrows of dreamland. There being nothing real to weigh them against, the trivial did duty for the great.

This period of my life, from the age of fifteen or sixteen to twenty-two or twenty-three, was one of utter disorderliness.

When, in the early ages of the Earth, land and water had not yet distinctly separated, huge misshapen amphibious creatures walked the trunkless forests growing on the oozing silt. Thus do the passions of the dim ages of the immature mind, as disproportionate and curiously shaped, haunt the unending shades of its trackless, nameless wildernesses. They know not themselves, nor the aim of their wanderings; and, because they do not, they are ever apt to imitate something else. So, at this age of unmeaning activity, when my undeveloped powers, unaware of and unequal to their object, were jostling each other for an outlet, each sought to assert superiority through exaggeration.

When milk-teeth are trying to push their way through, they work the infant into a fever. All this agitation finds no justification till the teeth are out and have begun assisting in the absorption of food. In the same way do our early passions torment the mind, like a malady, till they realise their true relationship with the outer world.

The lessons I learnt from my experiences at that stage are to be found in every moral textbook, but are not therefore to be despised. That which keeps our appetities confined within us, and checks their free access to the outside, poisons our life. Such is selfishness which refuses to give free play to our desires, and prevents them from reaching their real goal, and that is why it is always accompanied by festering untruths and extravagances. When our desires find unlimited freedom in good work they shake off their diseased condition and come back to their own nature;—that is their true end, there also is the joy of their being.

The condition of my immature mind which I have described was fostered both by the example and precept of the time, and I am not sure that the effects of these are not lingering on to the present day. Glancing back at the period of which I tell, it strikes me that we had gained more of stimulation than of nourishment out of English Literature. Our literary gods then were Shakespeare, Milton and Byron; and the quality in their work which stirred us most was strength of passion. In the social life of Englishmen passionate outbursts are kept severely in check, for which very reason, perhaps, they so dominate their literature, making its characteristic to be the working out of extravagantly vehement feelings to an inevitable conflagration. At least this uncontrolled excitement was what we learnt to look on as the quintessence of English literature.

In the impetuous declamation of English poetry by Akshay Chowdhury, our initiator into English

Moonlight

literature, there was the wildness of intoxication. The frenzy of Romeo's and Juliet's love, the fury of King Lear's impotent lamentation, the all-consuming fire of Othello's jealousy, these were the things that roused us to enthusiastic admiration. Our restricted social life, our narrower field of activity, was hedged in with such monotonous uniformity that tempestuous feelings found no entrance;—all was as calm and quiet as could be. So our hearts naturally craved the life-bringing shock of the passionate emotion in English literature. Ours was not the æsthetic enjoyment of literary art, but the jubilant welcome by stagnation of a turbulent wave, even though it should stir up to the surface the slime of the bottom.

Shakespeare's contemporary literature represents the war-dance of the day when the Renascence came to Europe in all the violence of its reaction against the severe curbing and cramping of the hearts of men. The examination of good and evil, beauty and ugliness, was not the main object,—man then seemed consumed with the anxiety to break through all barriers to the inmost sanctuary of his being, there to discover the ultimate image of his own violent desire. That is why in this literature we find such poignant, such exuberant, such unbridled expression.

The spirit of this bacchanalian revelry of Europe found entrance into our demurely well-behaved social world, woke us up, and made us lively. We were dazzled by the glow of unfettered life which fell upon our custom-smothered heart, pining for an opportunity to disclose itself.

There was another such day in English literature when the slow-measure of Pope's common time gave place to the dance-rhythm of the French revolution. This had Byron for its poet. And the impetuosity of his passion also moved our veiled heart-bride in the seclusion of her corner.

In this wise did the excitement of the pursuit of English literature come to sway the heart of the youth of our time, and at mine the waves of this excitement kept beating from every side. The first awakening is the time for the play of energy, not its repression.

And yet our case was so different from that of Europe. There the excitability and impatience of bondage was a reflection from its history into its literature. Its expression was consistent with its feeling. The roaring of the storm was heard because a storm was really raging. The breeze therefrom that ruffled our little world sounded in reality but little above a murmur. Therein it failed to satisfy our minds, so that our attempts to imitate the blast of a hurricane led us easily into exaggeration,—a tendency which still persists and may not prove easy of cure.

And for this, the fact that in English literature the reticence of true art has not yet appeared, is responsible. Human emotion is only one of the ingredients of literature and not its end,—which is the beauty of perfect fulness consisting in simplicity and restraint. This is a proposition which English literature does not yet fully admit.

Our minds from infancy to old age are being moulded by this English literature alone. But other literatures of Europe, both classical and modern, of which the art-form shows the well-nourished development due to a systematic cultivation of self-control, are not subjects of our study; and so, as it seems to me, we are yet unable to arrive at a correct perception of the true aim and method of literary work.

Akshay Babu, who had made the passion in English literature living to us, was himself a votary of the emotional life. The importance of realising truth in the fulness of its perfection seemed less apparent to him than that of feeling it in the heart. He had no intellectual respect for religion, but songs of *Shyāmā*, the dark Mother, would bring tears to his eyes. He felt no call to search for ultimate reality; whatever moved his heart served him for the time as the truth, even obvious coarseness not proving a deterrent.

Atheism was the dominant note of the English prose writings then in vogue,—Bentham, Mill and Comte being favourite authors. Theirs was the reasoning in terms of which our youths argued. The age of Mill constitutes a natural epoch in English History. It represents a healthy reaction of the body politic; these destructive forces having been brought in, temporarily, to rid it of accumulated thought-rubbish. In our country we received these in the letter, but never sought to make practical use of them, employing them only as a stimulant to incite ourselves to moral revolt. Atheism was thus for us a mere intoxication.

For these reasons educated men then fell mainly into two classes. One class would be always thrusting themselves forward with unprovoked argumentation to cut to pieces all belief in God. Like the hunter whose hands itch, no sooner he spies a living creature on the top or at the foot of a tree, to kill it, whenever these came to learn of a harmless belief lurking anywhere in fancied security, they felt stirred up to sally forth and demolish it. We had for a short time a tutor of whom this was a pet diversion. Though I was a mere boy, even I could not escape his onslaughts. Not that his attainments were of any account, or that his opinions were the result of any enthusiastic search for the truth, being mostly gathered from others' lips. But though I fought him with all my strength, unequally matched in age as we were, I suffered many a bitter defeat. Sometimes I felt so mortified I almost wanted to cry.

The other class consisted not of believers, but religious epicureans, who found comfort and solace in gathering together, and steeping themselves in pleasing sights, sounds and scents galore, under the garb of religious ceremonial; they luxuriated in the paraphernalia of worship. In neither of these classes was doubt or denial the outcome of the travail of their quest.

Though these religious aberrations pained me, I cannot say I was not at all influenced by them. With the intellectual impudence of budding youth this revolt also found a place. The religious services which were held in our family I would have nothing to do with, I had not accepted them for my own. I was busy blowing up a raging flame with the bellows of my emotions. It was only the worship of fire, the giving of oblations to increase its flame—with no other aim. And because my endeavour had no end in view it was measureless, always reaching beyond any assigned limit.

As with religion, so with my emotions, I felt no need for any underlying truth, my excitement being an end in itself. I call to mind some lines of a poet of that time:

> My heart is mine
> I have sold it to none,
> Be it tattered and torn and worn away,
> My heart is mine!

From the standpoint of truth the heart need not worry itself so; for nothing compels it to wear itself to tatters. In truth sorrow is not desirable, but taken apart its pungency may appear savoury. This savour our poets often made much of; leaving out the god in whose worship they were indulging. This childishness our country has not yet succeeded in getting rid of. So even to-day, when we fail to see the truth of religion, we seek in its observance an artistic gratification. So, also, much of our patriotism is not service of the mother-land, but the luxury of bringing ourselves into a desirable attitude of mind toward the country.

PART VI

(28) *European Music*

WHEN I was in Brighton I once went to hear some Prima Donna. I forget her name. It may have been Madame Neilson or Madame Albani. Never before had I come across such an extraordinary command over the voice. Even our best singers cannot hide their sense of effort; nor are they ashamed to bring out, as best they can, top notes or bass notes beyond their proper register. In our country the understanding portion of the audience think no harm in keeping the performance up to standard by dint of their own imagination. For the same reason they do not mind any harshness of voice or uncouthness of gesture in the exponent of a perfectly formed melody; on the contrary, they seem sometimes to be of opinion that such minor external defects serve better to set off the internal perfection of the composition,—as with the outward poverty of the Great Ascetic, Mahadeva, whose divinity shines forth naked.

This feeling seems entirely wanting in Europe. There, outward embellishment must be perfect in every detail, and the least defect stands shamed and unable to face the public gaze. In our musical gatherings nothing is thought of spending half-an-hour in tuning up the *Tanpuras*, or hammering into tone the drums, little and big. In Europe such duties are performed beforehand, behind the scenes, for all that comes in front must be faultless. There is thus no room for any weak spot in the singer's voice. In our country a correct and artistic exposition[1] of the melody is the main object, thereon is concentrated all the effort. In Europe the voice is the object of culture, and with it they perform impossibilities. In our country the virtuoso is satisfied if he has heard the song; in Europe, they go to hear the singer.

That is what I saw that day in Brighton. To me it was as good as a circus. But, admire the performance as I did, I could not appreciate the song. I could hardly keep from laughing when some of the *cadenzas* imitated the warbling of birds. I felt all the time that it was a misapplication of the human voice. When it came to the turn of a male singer I was considerably relieved. I specially liked the tenor voices which had more of human flesh and blood in them, and seemed less like the disembodied lament of a forlorn spirit.

After this, as I went on hearing and learning more and more of European music, I began to get

[1] With Indian music it is not a mere question of correctly rendering a melody exactly as composed, but the theme of the original composition is the subject of an improvised interpretative elaboration by the expounding Artist. *Tr.*

into the spirit of it; but up to now I am convinced that our music and theirs abide in altogether different apartments, and do not gain entry to the heart by the self-same door.

European music seems to be intertwined with its material life, so that the text of its songs may be as various as that life itself. If we attempt to put our tunes to the same variety of use they tend to lose their significance, and become ludicrous; for our melodies transcend the barriers of everyday life, and only thus can they carry us so deep into Pity, so high into Aloofness; their function being to reveal a picture of the inmost inexpressible depths of our being, mysterious and impenetrable, where the devotee may find his hermitage ready, or even the epicurean his bower, but where there is no room for the busy man of the world.

I cannot claim that I gained admittance to the soul of European music. But what little of it I came to understand from the outside attracted me greatly in one way. It seemed to me so romantic. It is somewhat difficult to analyse what I mean by that word. What I would refer to is the aspect of variety, of abundance, of the waves on the sea of life, of the ever-changing light and shade on their ceaseless undulations. There is the opposite aspect—of pure extension, of the unwinking blue of the sky, of the silent hint of immeasureability in the distant circle of the horizon. However that may be, let me repeat, at the risk of not being perfectly clear, that whenever I have been moved by European music I have said to myself: it is romantic, it is translating into melody the evanescence of life.

Not that we wholly lack the same attempt in some forms of our music; but it is less pronounced, less successful. Our melodies give voice to the star-spangled night, to the first reddening of dawn. They speak of the sky-pervading sorrow which lowers in the darkness of clouds; the speechless deep intoxication of the forest-roaming spring.

(29) *Valmiki Pratibha*

We had a profusely decorated volume of Moore's Irish Melodies: and often have I listened to the enraptured recitation of these by Akshay Babu. The poems combined with the pictorial designs to conjure up for me a dream picture of the Ireland of old. I had not then actually heard the original tunes, but had sung these Irish Melodies to myself to the accompaniment of the harps in the pictures. I longed to hear the real tunes, to learn them, and sing them to Akshay Babu. Some longings unfortunately do get fulfilled in this life, and die in the process. When I went to England I did hear some of the Irish Melodies sung, and learnt them too, but that put an end to my keenness to learn more. They were simple, mournful and sweet, but they somehow did not fit in with the silent melody of the harp which filled the halls of the Old Ireland of my dreams.

When I came back home I sung the Irish melodies I had learnt to my people. "What is the matter with Rabi's voice?" they exclaimed. "How funny and foreign it sounds!" They even felt my speaking voice had changed its tone.

From this mixed cultivation of foreign and native melody was born the *Valmiki Pratibha.*[1] The tunes in this musical drama are mostly Indian, but they have been dragged out of their classic dignity; that which soared in the sky was taught to run on the earth. Those who have seen and heard it performed will, I trust, bear witness that the harnessing of Indian melodic modes to the service of the drama has proved neither derogatory nor futile. This conjunction is the only special feature of *Valmiki Pratibha.* The pleasing task of loosening the chains of melodic forms and making

[1] Valmiki Pratibha means the genius of Valmiki. The plot is based on the story of Valmiki, the robber chief, being moved to pity and breaking out into a metrical lament on witnessing the grief of one of a pair of cranes whose mate was killed by a hunter. In the metre which so came to him he afterwards composed his *Ramayana. Tr.*

them adaptable to a variety of treatment completely engrossed me.

Several of the songs of *Valmiki Pratibha* were set to tunes originally severely classic in mode; some of the tunes were composed by my brother Jyotirindra; a few were adapted from European sources. The *Telena*[1] style of Indian modes specially lends itself to dramatic purposes and has been frequently utilized in this work. Two English tunes served for the drinking songs of the robber band, and an Irish melody for the lament of the wood nymphs.

Valmiki Pratibha is not a composition which will bear being read. Its significance is lost if it is not heard sung and seen acted. It is not what Europeans call an Opera, but a little drama set to music. That is to say, it is not primarily a musical composition. Very few of the songs are important or attractive by themselves; they all serve merely as the musical text of the play.

Before I went to England we occasionally used to have gatherings of literary men in our house, at which music, recitations and light refreshments

[1] Some Indian classic melodic compositions are designed on a scheme of accentuation, for which purpose the music is set, not to words, but to unmeaning notation-sounds representing drum-beats or plectrum-impacts which in Indian music are of a considerable variety of tone, each having its own sound-symbol. The *Telena* is one such style of composition. *Tr.*

were served up. After my return one more such gathering was held, which happened to be the last. It was for an entertainment in this connection that the *Valmiki Pratibha* was composed. I played *Valmiki* and my niece, Pratibha, took the part of *Saraswati*—which bit of history remains recorded in the name.

I had read in some work of Herbert Spencer's that speech takes on tuneful inflexions whenever emotion comes into play. It is a fact that the tone or tune is as important to us as the spoken word for the expression of anger, sorrow, joy and wonder. Spencer's idea that, through a development of these emotional modulations of voice, man found music, appealed to me. Why should it not do, I thought to myself, to act a drama in a kind of recitative based on this idea. The *Kathakas* [1] of our country attempt this to some extent, for they frequently break into a chant which, however, stops short of full melodic form. As blank verse is more elastic than rhymed, so such chanting, though not devoid of rhythm, can more freely adapt itself to the emotional interpretation of the text, because it does not attempt to conform to the more rigorous canons of tune and time required by a regular melodic composition. The expression of feeling being the object, these de-

[1] Reciters of Puranic legendary lore. *Tr.*

ficiencies in regard to form do not jar on the hearer.

Encouraged by the success of this new line taken in the *Valmiki Pratibha*, I composed another musical play of the same class. It was called the *Kal Mrigaya*, The Fateful Hunt. The plot was based on the story of the accidental killing of the blind hermit's only son by King Dasaratha. It was played on a stage erected on our roof-terrace, and the audience seemed profoundly moved by its pathos. Afterwards, much of it was, with slight changes, incorporated in the *Valmiki Pratibha*, and this play ceased to be separately published in my works.

Long afterwards, I composed a third muscial play, *Mayar Khela*, the Play of *Maya*, an operetta of a different type. In this the songs were important, not the drama. In the others a series of dramatic situations were strung on a thread of melody; this was a garland of songs with just a thread of dramatic plot running through. The play of feeling, and not action, was its special feature. In point of fact I was, while composing it, saturated with the mood of song.

The enthusiasm which went to the making of *Valmiki Pratibha* and *Kal Mrigaya* I have never felt for any other work of mine. In these two the creative musical impulse of the time found expression.

My brother, Jyotirindra, was engaged the livelong day at his piano, refashioning the classic melodic forms at his pleasure. And, at every turn of his instrument, the old modes took on unthought-of shapes and expressed new shades of feeling. The melodic forms which had become habituated to their pristine stately gait, when thus compelled to march to more lively unconventional measures, displayed an unexpected agility and power; and moved us correspondingly. We could plainly hear the tunes speak to us while Akshay Babu and I sat on either side fitting words to them as they grew out of my brother's nimble fingers. I do not claim that our *libretto* was good poetry but it served as a vehicle for the tunes.

In the riotous joy of this revolutionary activity were these two musical plays composed, and so they danced merrily to every measure, whether or not technically correct, indifferent as to the tunes being homelike or foreign.

On many an occasion has the Bengali reading public been grievously exercised over some opinion or literary form of mine, but it is curious to find that the daring with which I had played havoc with accepted musical notions did not rouse any resentment; on the contrary those who came to hear departed pleased. A few of Akshay Babu's compositions find place in the *Valmiki Pratibha* and also adaptations from Vihari Chakravarti's *Sarada Mangal* series of songs.

I used to take the leading part in the performance of these musical dramas. From my early years I had a taste for acting, and firmly believed that I had a special aptitude for it. I think I proved that my belief was not ill-founded. I had only once before done the part of Aleek Babu in a farce written by my brother Jyotirindra. So these were really my first attempts at acting. I was then very young and nothing seemed to fatigue or trouble my voice.

In our house, at the time, a cascade of musical emotion was gushing forth day after day, hour after hour, its scattered spray reflecting into our being a whole gamut of rainbow colours. Then, with the freshness of youth, our new-born energy, impelled by its virgin curiosity, struck out new paths in every direction. We felt we would try and test everything, and no achievement seemed impossible. We wrote, we sang, we acted, we poured ourselves out on every side. This was how I stepped into my twentieth year.

Of these forces which so triumphantly raced our lives along, my brother Jyotirindra was the charioteer. He was absolutely fearless. Once, when I was a mere lad, and had never ridden a horse before, he made me mount one and gallop by his side, with no qualms about his unskilled companion. When at the same age, while we were at Shelidah, (the head-quarters of our estate,) news was brought of a tiger, he took me with him on a hunting expedition. I had no gun,—it would have been more dangerous to me than to the tiger if I had. We left our shoes at the outskirts of the jungle and crept in with bare feet. At last we scrambled up into a bamboo thicket, partly stripped of its thorn-like twigs, where I somehow managed to crouch behind my brother till the deed was done; with no means of even administering a shoe-beating to the unmannerly brute had he dared lay his offensive paws on me!

Thus did my brother give me full freedom both internal and external in the face of all dangers. No usage or custom was a bondage for him, and so was he able to rid me of my shrinking diffidence.

(30) *Evening Songs*

In the state of being confined within myself, of which I have been telling, I wrote a number of poems which have been grouped together, under the title of the *Heart-Wilderness*, in Mohita Babu's edition of my works. In one of the poems subsequently published in a volume called *Morning Songs*, the following lines occur:

There is a vast wilderness whose name is *Heart;*
Whose interlacing forest branches dandle and rock darkness like an infant.
I lost my way in its depths.

from which came the idea of the name for this group of poems.

Much of what I wrote, when thus my life had no commerce with the outside, when I was engrossed in the contemplation of my own heart, when my imaginings wandered in many a disguise amidst causeless emotions and aimless longings, has been left out of that edition; only a few of the poems originally published in the volume entitled *Evening Songs* finding a place there, in the *Heart-Wilderness* group.

My brother Jyotirindra and his wife had left home travelling on a long journey, and their rooms on the third storey, facing the terraced-roof, were empty. I took possession of these and the terrace, and spent my days in solitude. While thus left in communion with my self alone, I know not how I slipped out of the poetical groove into which I had fallen. Perhaps being cut off from those whom I sought to please, and whose taste in poetry moulded the form I tried to put my thoughts into, I naturally gained freedom from the style they had imposed on me.

I began to use a slate for my writing. That also

helped in my emancipation. The manuscript books in which I had indulged before seemed to demand a certain height of poetic flight, to work up to which I had to find my way by a comparison with others. But the slate was clearly fitted for my mood of the moment. "Fear not," it seemed to say. "Write just what you please, one rub will wipe all away!"

As I wrote a poem or two, thus unfettered, I felt a great joy well up within me. "At last," said my heart, "what I write is my own!" Let no one mistake this for an accession of pride. Rather did I feel a pride in my former productions, as being all the tribute I had to pay them. But I refuse to call the realisation of self, self-sufficiency. The joy of parents in their first-born is not due to any pride in its appearance, but because it is their very own. If it happens to be an extraordinary child they may also glory in that—but that is different.

In the first flood-tide of that joy I paid no heed to the bounds of metrical form, and as the stream does not flow straight on but winds about as it lists, so did my verse. Before, I would have held this to be a crime, but now I felt no compunction. Freedom first breaks the law and then makes laws which brings it under true Self-rule.

The only listener I had for these erratic poems of mine was Akshay Babu. When he heard them for the first time he was as surprised as he was pleased, and with his approbation my road to freedom was widened.

The poems of Vihari Chakravarti were in a 3-beat metre. This triple time produces a rounded-off globular effect, unlike the square-cut multiple of 2. It rolls on with ease, it glides as it dances to the tinkling of its anklets. I was once very fond of this metre. It felt more like riding a bicycle than walking. And to this stride I had got accustomed. In the *Evening Songs*, without thinking of it, I somehow broke off this habit. Nor did I come under any other particular bondage. I felt entirely free and unconcerned. I had no thought or fear of being taken to task.

The strength I gained by working, freed from the trammels of tradition, led me to discover that I had been searching in impossible places for that which I had within myself. Nothing but want of self-confidence had stood in the way of my coming into my own. I felt like rising from a dream of bondage to find myself unshackled. I cut extraordinary capers just to make sure I was free to move.

To me this is the most memorable period of my poetic career. As poems my *Evening Songs* may not have been worth much, in fact as such they are crude enough. Neither their metre, nor language, nor thought had taken definite shape. Their only merit is that for the first time I had come to write what I really meant, just according to my pleasure. What if those compositions have no value, that pleasure certainly had.

(31) *An Essay on Music*

I had been proposing to study for the bar when my father had recalled me home from England. Some friends concerned at this cutting short of my career pressed him to send me off once again. This led to my starting on a second voyage towards England, this time with a relative as my companion. My fate, however, had so strongly vetoed my being called to the bar that I was not even to reach England this time. For a certain reason we had to disembark at Madras and return home to Calcutta. The reason was by no means as grave as its outcome, but as the laugh was not against *me*, I refrain from setting it down here. From both my attempted pilgrimages to *Lakshmi's* [1] shrine I had thus to come back repulsed. I hope, however, that the Law-god, at least, will look on me with a favourable eye for that I have not added to the encumbrances on the Bar-library premises.

My father was then in the Mussoorie hills. I

[1] The Goddess of Wealth.

went to him in fear and trembling. But he showed no sign of irritation, he rather seemed pleased. He must have seen in this return of mine the blessing of Divine Providence.

The evening before I started on this voyage I read a paper at the Medical College Hall on the invitation of the Bethune Society. This was my first public reading. The Reverend K. M. Banerji was the president. The subject was Music. Leaving aside instrumental music, I tried to make out that to bring out better what the words sought to express was the chief end and aim of vocal music. The text of my paper was but meagre. I sang and acted songs throughout illustrating my theme. The only reason for the flattering eulogy which the President bestowed on me at the end must have been the moving effect of my young voice together with the earnestness and variety of its efforts. But I must make the confession to-day that the opinion I voiced with such enthusiasm that evening was wrong.

The art of vocal music has its own special functions and features. And when it happens to be set to words the latter must not presume too much on their opportunity and seek to supersede the melody of which they are but the vehicle. The song being great in its own wealth, why should it wait upon the words? Rather does it begin where mere words fail. Its power lies in the region of the inexpressible; it tells us what the words cannot.

So the less a song is burdened with words the better. In the classic style of Hindustan [1] the words are of no account and leave the melody to make its appeal in its own way. Vocal music reaches its perfection when the melodic form is allowed to develop freely, and carry our consciousness with it to its own wonderful plane. In Bengal, however, the words have always asserted themselves so, that our provincial song has failed to develop her full musical capabilities, and has remained content as the handmaiden of her sister art of poetry. From the old *Vaishnava* songs down to those of Nidhu Babu she has displayed her charms from the background. But as in our country the wife rules her husband through acknowledging her dependence, so our music, though professedly in attendance only, ends by dominating the song.

I have often felt this while composing my songs. As I hummed to myself and wrote the lines:

> Do not keep your secret to yourself, my love,
> But whisper it gently to me, only to me.

I found that the words had no means of reaching by themselves the region into which they were

[1] As distinguished generally from different provincial styles, but chiefly from the Dravidian style prevalent in the South. *Tr.*

borne away by the tune. The melody told me that the secret, which I was so importunate to hear, had mingled with the green mystery of the forest glades, was steeped in the silent whiteness of moonlight nights, peeped out of the veil of the illimitable blue behind the horizon—and is the one intimate secret of Earth, Sky and Waters.

In my early boyhood I heard a snatch of a song:

> Who dressed you, love, as a foreigner?

This one line painted such wonderful pictures in my mind that it haunts me still. One day I sat down to set to words a composition of my own while full of this bit of song. Humming my tune I wrote to its accompaniment:

> I know you, O Woman from the strange land!
> Your dwelling is across the Sea.

Had the tune not been there I know not what shape the rest of the poem might have taken; but the magic of the melody revealed to me the stranger in all her loveliness. It is she, said my soul, who comes and goes, a messenger to this world from the other shore of the ocean of mystery. It is she, of whom we now and again catch glimpses in the dewy Autumn mornings, in the scented nights of Spring, in the inmost recesses of our hearts—and sometimes we strain skywards to hear her song. To the door of this world-charming stranger the melody, as I say, wafted me, and so to her were the rest of the words addressed.

Long after this, in a street in Bolpur, a mendicant *Baul* was singing as he walked along:

How does the unknown bird flit in and out of the cage!
Ah, could I but catch it, I'd ring its feet with my love!

I found this *Baul* to be saying the very same thing. The unknown bird sometimes surrenders itself within the bars of the cage to whisper tidings of the bondless unknown beyond. The heart would fain hold it near to itself for ever, but cannot. What but the melody of song can tell us of the goings and comings of the unknown bird?

That is why I am always reluctant to publish books of the words of songs, for therein the soul must needs be lacking.

(32) *The River-side*

When I returned home from the outset of my second voyage to England, my brother Jyotirindra and sister-in-law were living in a river-side villa at Chandernagore, and there I went to stay with them.

The Ganges again! Again those ineffable days and nights, languid with joy, sad with longing, attuned to the plaintive babbling of the river along the cool shade of its wooded banks. This Bengal sky-full of light, this south breeze, this flow of the river, this right royal laziness, this broad leisure stretching from horizon to horizon and from green earth to blue sky, all these were to me as food and drink to the hungry and thirsty. Here it felt indeed like home, and in these I recognised the ministrations of a Mother.

That was not so very long ago, and yet time has wrought many changes. Our little river-side nests, clustering under their surrounding greenery, have been replaced by mills which now, dragon-like, everywhere rear their hissing heads, belching forth black smoke. In the midday glare of modern life even our hours of mental siesta have been narrowed down to the lowest limit, and hydra-headed unrest has invaded every department of life. Maybe, this is for the better, but I, for one, cannot account it wholly to the good.

These lovely days of mine at the riverside passed by like so many dedicated lotus blossoms floating down the sacred stream. Some rainy afternoons I spent in a veritable frenzy, singing away old *Vaishnava* songs to my own tunes, accompanying myself on a harmonium. On other afternoons, we would drift along in a boat, my brother Jyotirindra accompanying my singing with his violin. And as,

The Ganges Again

beginning with the *Puravi*,[1] we went on varying the mode of our music with the declining day, we saw, on reaching the *Behaga*,[1] the western sky close the doors of its factory of golden toys, and the moon on the east rise over the fringe of trees.

Then we would row back to the landing steps of the villa and seat ourselves on a quilt spread on the terrace facing the river. By then a silvery peace rested on both land and water, hardly any boats were about, the fringe of trees on the bank was reduced to a deep shadow, and the moonlight glimmered over the smooth flowing stream.

The villa we were living in was known as 'Moran's Garden'. A flight of stone-flagged steps led up from the water to a long, broad verandah which formed part of the house. The rooms were not regularly arranged, nor all on the same level, and some had to be reached by short flights of stairs. The big sitting room overlooking the landing steps had stained glass windows with coloured pictures.

One of the pictures was of a swing hanging from a branch half-hidden in dense foliage, and in the checkered light and shade of this bower, two persons were swinging; and there was another of a broad flight of steps leading into some castle-like

[1] Many of the Hindustani classic modes are supposed to be best in keeping with particular seasons of the year, or times of the day. *Tr.*

palace, up and down which men and women in festive garb were going and coming. When the light fell on the windows, these pictures shone wonderfully, seeming to fill the river-side atmosphere with holiday music. Some far-away long-forgotten revelry seemed to be expressing itself in silent words of light; the love thrills of the swinging couple making alive with their eternal story the woodlands of the river bank.

The topmost room of the house was in a round tower with windows opening to every side. This I used as my room for writing poetry. Nothing could be seen from thence save the tops of the surrounding trees, and the open sky. I was then busy with the *Evening Songs* and of this room I wrote:

There, where in the breast of limitless space clouds are laid to sleep,
I have built my house for thee, O Poesy!

(33) *More About the Evening Songs*

At this time my reputation amongst literary critics was that of being a poet of broken cadence and lisping utterance. Everything about my work was dubbed misty, shadowy. However little I might have relished this at the time, the charge was not wholly baseless. My poetry did in fact lack the backbone of worldly reality. How, amidst the ringed-in seclusion of my early years, was I to get the necessary material?

But one thing I refuse to admit. Behind this charge of vagueness was the sting of the insinuation of its being a deliberate affectation—for the sake of effect. The fortunate possessor of good eye-sight is apt to sneer at the youth with glasses, as if he wears them for ornament. While a reflection on the poor fellow's infirmity may be permissible, it is too bad to charge him with pretending not to see.

The nebula is not an outside creation—it merely represents a phase; and to leave out all poetry which has not attained definiteness would not bring us to the truth of literature. If any phase of man's nature has found true expression, it is worth preserving—it may be cast aside only if not expressed truly. There is a period in man's life when his feelings are the pathos of the inexpressible, the anguish of vagueness. The poetry which attempts its expression cannot be called baseless—at worst it may be worthless; but it is not necessarily even that. The sin is not in the thing expressed, but in the failure to express it.

There is a duality in man. Of the inner person, behind the outward current of thoughts, feelings and events, but little is known or recked; but for all that, he cannot be got rid of as a factor in life's progress. When the outward life fails to harmonise with the inner, the dweller within is hurt, and his pain manifests itself in the outer consciousness in a manner to which it is difficult to give a name, or even to describe, and of which the cry is more akin to an inarticulate wail than words with more precise meaning.

The sadness and pain which sought expression in the *Evening Songs* had their roots in the depths of my being. As one's sleep-smothered consciousness wrestles with a nightmare in its efforts to awake, so the submerged inner self struggles to free itself from its complexities and come out into the open. These *Songs* are the history of that struggle. As in all creation, so in poetry, there is the opposition of forces. If the divergence is too wide, or the unison too close, there is, it seems to me, no room for poetry. Where the pain of discord strives to attain and express its resolution into harmony, there does poetry break forth into music, as breath through a flute.

When the *Evening Songs* first saw the light they were not hailed with any flourish of trumpets, but none the less they did not lack admirers. I have elsewhere told the story of how at the wedding of Mr. Ramesh Chandra Dutt's eldest daughter, Bankim Babu was at the door, and the host was welcoming him with the customary garland of flowers. As I came up Bankim Babu eagerly took the garland and placing it round my neck said: "The wreath to him, Ramesh, have you not read his *Evening Songs?*" And when Mr. Dutt avowed he had not yet done so, the manner in which Bankim Babu expressed his opinion of some of them amply rewarded me.

The *Evening Songs* gained for me a friend whose approval, like the rays of the sun, stimulated and guided the shoots of my newly sprung efforts. This was Babu Priyanath Sen. Just before this the *Broken Heart* had led him to give up all hopes of me. I won him back with these *Evening Songs*. Those who are acquainted with him know him as an expert navigator of all the seven seas [1] of literature, whose highways and byways, in almost all languages, Indian and foreign, he is constantly traversing. To converse with him is to gain glimpses of even the most out of the way scenery in the world of ideas. This proved of the greatest value to me.

He was able to give his literary opinions with the fullest confidence, for he had not to rely on his unaided taste to guide his likes and dislikes. This authoritative criticism of his also assisted

[1] The world, as the Indian boy knows it from fairy tale and folklore, has seven seas and thirteen rivers. *Tr.*

me more than I can tell. I used to read to him everything I wrote, and but for the timely showers of his discriminate appreciation it is hard to say whether these early ploughings of mine would have yielded as they have done.

(34) *Morning Songs*

At the river-side I also did a bit of prose writing, not on any definite subject or plan, but in the spirit that boys catch butterflies. When spring comes within, many-coloured short-lived fancies are born and flit about in the mind, ordinarily unnoticed. In these days of my leisure, it was perhaps the mere whim to collect them which had come upon me. Or it may have been only another phase of my emancipated self which had thrown out its chest and decided to write just as it pleased; what I wrote not being the object, it being sufficient unto itself that it was I who wrote. These prose pieces were published later under the name of *Vividha Prabandha*, Various Topics, but they expired with the first edition and did not get a fresh lease of life in a second.

At this time, I think, I also began my first novel, *Bauthakuranir Hat*.

After we had stayed for a time by the river, my brother Jyotirindra took a house in Calcutta, on Sudder Street near the Museum. I remained with him. While I went on here with the novel and the *Evening Songs*, a momentous revolution of some kind came about within me.

One day, late in the afternoon, I was pacing the terrace of our Jorasanko house. The glow of the sunset combined with the wan twilight in a way which seemed to give the approaching evening a specially wonderful attractiveness for me. Even the walls of the adjoining house seemed to grow beautiful. Is this uplifting of the cover of triviality from the everyday world, I wondered, due to some magic in the evening light? Never!

I could see at once that it was the effect of the evening which had come within me; its shades had obliterated my *self*. While the self was rampant during the glare of day, everything I perceived was mingled with and hidden by it. Now, that the self was put into the background, I could see the world in its own true aspect. And that aspect has nothing of triviality in it, it is full of beauty and joy.

Since this experience I tried the effect of deliberately suppressing my *self* and viewing the world as a mere spectator, and was invariably rewarded with a sense of special pleasure. I remember I tried also to explain to a relative how to see the world in its true light, and the incidental lightening of one's own sense of burden which follows such vision; but, as I believe, with no success.

Then I gained a further insight which has lasted all my life.

The end of Sudder Street, and the trees on the Free School grounds opposite, were visible from our Sudder Street house. One morning I happened to be standing on the verandah looking that way. The sun was just rising through the leafy tops of those trees. As I continued to gaze, all of a sudden a covering seemed to fall away from my eyes, and I found the world bathed in a wonderful radiance, with waves of beauty and joy swelling on every side. This radiance pierced in a moment through the folds of sadness and despondency which had accumulated over my heart, and flooded it with this universal light.

That very day the poem, *The Awakening of the Waterfall*, gushed forth and coursed on like a veritable cascade. The poem came to an end, but the curtain did not fall upon the joy aspect of the Universe. And it came to be so that no person or thing in the world seemed to me trivial or unpleasing. A thing that happened the next day or the day following seemed specially astonishing.

There was a curious sort of person who came

to me now and then, with a habit of asking all manner of silly questions. One day he had asked: "Have you, sir, seen God with your own eyes?" And on my having to admit that I had not, he averred that he had. "What was it you saw?" I asked. "He seethed and throbbed before my eyes!" was the reply.

It can well be imagined that one would not ordinarily relish being drawn into abstruse discussions with such a person. Moreover, I was at the time entirely absorbed in my own writing. Nevertheless as he was a harmless sort of fellow I did not like the idea of hurting his susceptibilities and so tolerated him as best I could.

This time, when he came one afternoon, I actually felt glad to see him, and welcomed him cordially. The mantle of his oddity and foolishness seemed to have slipped off, and the person I so joyfully hailed was the real man whom I felt to be in nowise inferior to myself, and moreover closely related. Finding no trace of annoyance within me at sight of him, nor any sense of my time being wasted with him, I was filled with an immense gladness, and felt rid of some enveloping tissue of untruth which had been causing me so much needless and uncalled for discomfort and pain.

As I would stand on the balcony, the gait, the

figure, the features of each one of the passers-by, whoever they might be, seemed to me all so extraordinarily wonderful, as they flowed past,—waves on the sea of the universe. From infancy I had seen only with my eyes, I now began to see with the whole of my consciousness. I could not look upon the sight of two smiling youths, nonchalantly going their way, the arm of one on the other's shoulder, as a matter of small moment; for, through it I could see the fathomless depths of the eternal spring of Joy from which numberless sprays of laughter leap up throughout the world.

I had never before marked the play of limbs and lineaments which always accompanies even the least of man's actions; now I was spell-bound by their variety, which I came across on all sides, at every moment. Yet I saw them not as being apart by themselves, but as parts of that amazingly beautiful greater dance which goes on at this very moment throughout the world of men, in each of their homes, in their multifarious wants and activities.

Friend laughs with friend, the mother fondles her child, one cow sidles up to another and licks its body, and the immeasurability behind these comes direct to my mind with a shock which almost savours of pain.

When of this period I wrote:

> I know not how of a sudden my heart flung open its doors,
> And let the crowd of worlds rush in, greeting each other,—

it was no poetic exaggeration. Rather I had not the power to express all I felt.

For some time together I remained in this self-forgetful state of bliss. Then my brother thought of going to the Darjeeling hills. So much the better, thought I. On the vast Himalayan tops I shall be able to see more deeply into what has been revealed to me in Sudder Street; at any rate I shall see how the Himayalas display themselves to my new gift of vision.

But the victory was with that little house in Sudder Street. When, after ascending the mountains, I looked around, I was at once aware I had lost my new vision. My sin must have been in imagining that I could get still more of truth from the outside. However sky-piercing the king of mountains may be, he can have nothing in his gift for me; while He who is the Giver can vouchsafe a vision of the eternal universe in the dingiest of lanes, and in a moment of time.

I wandered about amongst the firs, I sat near the falls and bathed in their waters, I gazed at the grandeur of Kinchinjunga through a cloudless sky, but in what had seemed to me these likeliest of places, I found *it* not. I had come to know it, but could see it no longer. While I was admiring the gem the lid had suddenly closed, leaving me staring at the enclosing casket. But, for all the attractiveness of its workmanship, there was no longer any danger of my mistaking it for merely an empty box.

My *Morning Songs* came to an end, their last echo dying out with *The Echo* which I wrote at Darjeeling. This apparently proved such an abstruse affair that two friends laid a wager as to its real meaning. My only consolation was that, as I was equally unable to explain the enigma to them when they came to me for a solution, neither of them had to lose any money over it. Alas! The days when I wrote excessively plain poems about *The Lotus* and *A Lake* had gone forever.

But does one write poetry to explain any matter? What is felt within the heart tries to find outside shape as a poem. So when after listening to a poem anyone says he has not understood, I feel nonplussed. If someone smells a flower and says he does not understand, the reply to him is: there is nothing to understand, it is only a scent. If he persists, saying: *that* I know, but what does it all *mean?* Then one has either to change the subject, or make it more abstruse by saying that the scent is the shape which the universal joy takes in the flower.

That words have meanings is just the difficulty. That is why the poet has to turn and twist them in metre and verse, so that the meaning may be held somewhat in check, and the feeling allowed a chance to express itself.

This utterance of feeling is not the statement of a fundamental truth, or a scientific fact, or a useful moral precept. Like a tear or a smile it is but a picture of what is taking place within. If Science or Philosophy may gain anything from it they are welcome, but that is not the reason of its being. If while crossing a ferry you can catch a fish you are a lucky man, but that does not make the ferry boat a fishing boat, nor should you abuse the ferryman if he does not make fishing his business.

The Echo was written so long ago that it has escaped attention and I am now no longer called upon to render an account of its meaning. Nevertheless, whatever its other merits or defects may be, I can assure my readers that it was not my intention to propound a riddle, or insidiously convey any erudite teaching. The fact of the matter was that a longing had been born within my heart, and, unable to find any other name, I had called the thing I desired an Echo.

When from the original fount in the depths of the Universe streams of melody are sent forth abroad, their echo is reflected into our heart from the faces of our beloved and the other beauteous things around us. It must be, as I suggested, this Echo which we love, and not the things themselves from which it happens to be reflected; for that which one day we scarce deign to glance at, may be, on another, the very thing which claims our whole devotion.

I had so long viewed the world with external vision only, and so had been unable to see its universal aspect of joy. When of a sudden, from some innermost depth of my being, a ray of light found its way out, it spread over and illuminated for me the whole universe, which then no longer appeared like heaps of things and happenings, but was disclosed to my sight as one whole. This experience seemed to tell me of the stream of melody issuing from the very heart of the universe and spreading over space and time, re-echoing thence as waves of joy which flow right back to the source.

When the artist sends his song forth from the depths of a full heart that is joy indeed. And the joy is redoubled when this same song is wafted back to him as hearer. If, when the creation of the Arch-Poet is thus returning back to him in a flood of joy, we allow it to flow over our consciousness, we at once, immediately, become aware, in an inexpressible manner, of the end to which this flood is streaming. And as we become aware our love goes forth; and our *selves* are moved from their moorings and would fain float down the stream of joy to its infinite goal. This is the meaning of the longing which stirs within us at the sight of Beauty.

The stream which comes from the Infinite and flows toward the finite—that is the True, the Good; it is subject to laws, definite in form. Its echo which returns towards the Infinite is Beauty and Joy; which are difficult to touch or grasp, and so make us beside ourselves. This is what I tried to say by way of a parable or a song in *The Echo*. That the result was not clear is not to be wondered at, for neither was the attempt then clear unto itself.

Let me set down here part of what I wrote in a letter, at a more advanced age, about the *Morning Songs*.

"There is none in the World, all are in my heart"—is a state of mind belonging to a particular age. When the heart is first awakened it puts forth its arms and would grasp the whole world, like the teething infant which thinks everything meant for its mouth. Gradually it comes to understand what it really wants and what it does not. Then do its nebulous emanations shrink upon themselves, get heated, and heat in their turn.

To begin by wanting the whole world is to get nothing. When desire is concentrated, with the whole strength of one's being upon any one object whatsoever it might be, then does the gateway to the Infinite become visible. The morning songs were the first throwing forth of my inner self outwards, and consequently they lack any signs of such concentration.

This all-pervading joy of a first outflow, however, has the effect of leading us to an acquaintance with the particular. The lake in its fulness seeks an outlet as a river. In this sense the permanent later love is narrower than first love. It is more definite in the direction of its activities, desires to realise the whole in each of its parts, and is thus impelled on towards the infinite. What it finally reaches is no longer the former indefinite extension of the heart's own inner joy, but a merging in the infinite reality which was outside itself, and thereby the attainment of the complete truth of its own longings.

In Mohita Babu's edition these *Morning Songs* have been placed in the group of poems entitled *Nishkraman*, The Emergence. For in these was to be found the first news of my coming out of the *Heart Wilderness* into the open world. Thereafter did this pilgrim heart make its acquaintance with that world, bit by bit, part by part, in many a mood and manner. And at the end, after gliding past all the numerous landing steps of ever-changing impermanence, it will reach the infinite,—not the vagueness of indeterminate possibility, but the consummation of perfect fulness of Truth.

From my earliest years I enjoyed a simple and intimate communion with Nature. Each one of the cocoanut trees in our garden had for me a distinct personality. When, on coming home from the Normal School, I saw behind the skyline of our roof-terrace blue-grey water-laden clouds thickly banked up, the immense depth of gladness which filled me, all in a moment, I can recall clearly even now. On opening my eyes every morning, the blithely awakening world used to call me to join it like a playmate; the perfervid noonday sky, during the long silent watches of the siesta hours, would spirit me away from the work-a-day world into the recesses of its hermit cell; and the darkness of night would open the door to its phantom paths, and take me over all the seven seas and thirteen rivers, past all possibilities and impossibilities, right into its wonderland.

Then one day, when, with the dawn of youth, my hungry heart began to cry out for its sustenance, a barrier was set up between this play of inside and outside. And my whole being eddied round and round my troubled heart, creating a vortex within itself, in the whirls of which its consciousness was confined.

This loss of the harmony between inside and outside, due to the over-riding claims of the heart in its hunger, and consequent restriction of the privilege of communion which had been mine, was mourned by me in the *Evening Songs*. In the *Morning Songs* I celebrated the sudden opening of a gate in the barrier, by what shock I know not, through which I regained the lost one, not only as I knew it before, but more deeply, more fully, by force of the intervening separation.

Thus did the First Book of my life come to an end with these chapters of union, separation and reunion. Or, rather, it is not true to say it has come to an end. The same subject has still to be continued through more elaborate solutions of worse complexities, to a greater conclusion. Each one comes here to finish but one book of life, which, during the progress of its various parts, grows spiral-wise on an ever-increasing radius. So, while each segment may appear different from the others at a cursory glance, they all really lead back to the self-same starting centre.

The prose writings of the *Evening Songs* period were published, as I have said, under the name of *Vividha Prabandha*. Those others which correspond to the time of my writing the *Morning Songs* came out under the title of *Alochana*, Discussions. The difference between the characteristics of these two would be a good index of the nature of the change that had in the meantime taken place within me.

PART VII

(35) *Rajendrahal Mitra*

IT was about this time that my brother Jyotirindra had the idea of founding a Literary Academy by bringing together all the men of letters of repute. To compile authoritative technical terms for the Bengali language and in other ways to assist in its growth was to be its object—therein differing but little from the lines on which the modern *Sahitya Parishat*, Academy of Literature, has taken shape.

Dr. Rajendrahal Mitra took up the idea of this Academy with enthusiasm, and he was eventually its president for the short time it lasted. When I went to invite Pandit Vidyasagar to join it, he gave a hearing to my explanation of its objects and the names of the proposed members, then said: "My advice to you is to leave us out—you will never accomplish anything with big wigs; they can never be got to agree with one another." With which he refused to come in. Bankim Babu became a member, but I cannot say that he took much interest in the work.

To be plain, so long as this academy lived Rajendrahal Mitra did everything singlehanded. He began with Geographical terms. The draft list was made out by Dr. Rajendrahal himself and was printed and circulated for the suggestions of the members. We had also an idea of transliterating in Bengali the name of each foreign country as pronounced by itself.

Pandit Vidyasagar's prophecy was fulfilled. It did not prove possible to get the big wigs to do anything. And the academy withered away shortly after sprouting. But Rajendrahal Mitra was an all-round expert and was an academy in himself. My labours in this cause were more than repaid by the privilege of his acquaintance. I have met many Bengali men of letters in my time but none who left the impression of such brilliance.

I used to go and see him in the office of the Court of Wards in Maniktala. I would go in the mornings and always find him busy with his studies, and with the inconsiderateness of youth, I felt no hesitation in disturbing him. But I have never seen him the least bit put out on that account. As soon as he saw me he would put aside his work and begin to talk to me. It is a matter of common knowledge that he was somewhat hard of hearing, so he hardly ever gave me occasion to put him any question. He would take up some broad subject and talk away upon it, and it was the attraction of these discourses which drew me there. Converse with no other person ever gave me such a wealth of suggestive ideas on so many different subjects. I would listen enraptured.

I think he was a member of the text-book committee and every book he received for approval, he read through and annotated in pencil. On some occasions he would select one of these books for the text of discourses on the construction of the Bengali language in particular or Philology in general, which were of the greatest benefit to me. There were few subjects which he had not studied and anything he had studied he could clearly expound.

If we had not relied on the other members of the Academy we had tried to found, but left everything to Dr. Rajendrahal, the present *Sahitya Parishat* would have doubtless found the matters it is now occupied with left in a much more advanced state by that one man alone.

Dr. Rajendrahal Mitra was not only a profound scholar, but he had likewise a striking personality which shone through his features. Full of fire as he was in his public life, he could also unbend graciously so as to talk on the most difficult subjects to a stripling like myself without any trace of a patronising tone. I even took advantage of his condescension to the extent of getting a contribution, *Yama's Dog*, from him for the

Bharabi. There were other great contemporaries of his with whom I would not have ventured to take such liberties, nor would I have met with the like response if I had.

And yet when he was on the war path his opponents on the Municipal Corporation or the Senate of the University were mortally afraid of him. In those days Kristo Das Pal was the tactful politician, and Rajendrahal Mitra the valiant fighter.

For the purposes of the Asiatic Society's publications and researches, he had to employ a number of Sanscrit Pandits to do the mechanical work for him. I remember how this gave certain envious and mean-minded detractors the opportunity of saying that everything was really done by these Pandits while Rajendrahal fraudulently appropriated all the credit. Even to-day we very often find the tools arrogating to themselves the lion's share of the achievement, imagining the wielder to be a mere ornamental figurehead. If the poor pen had a mind it would as certainly have bemoaned the unfairness of its getting all the stain and the writer all the glory!

It is curious that this extraordinary man should have got no recognition from his countrymen even after his death. One of the reasons may be that the national mourning for Vidyasagar, whose death followed shortly after, left no room for a recognition of the other bereavement. Another reason may be that his main contributions being outside the pale of Bengali literature, he had been unable to reach the heart of the people.

(36) *Karwar*

Our Sudder Street party next transferred itself to Karwar on the West Sea coast. Karwar is the headquarters of the Kanara district in the Southern portion of the Bombay Presidency. It is the tract of the Malaya Hills of Sanskrit literature where grow the cardamum creeper and the Sandal Tree. My second brother was then Judge there.

The little harbour, ringed round with hills, is so secluded that it has nothing of the aspect of a port about it. Its crescent shaped beach throws out its arms to the shoreless open sea like the very image of an eager striving to embrace the infinite. The edge of the broad sandy beach is fringed with a forest of casuarinas, broken at one end by the *Kalanadi* river which here flows into the sea after passing through a gorge flanked by rows of hills on either side.

I remember how one moonlit evening we went up this river in a little boat. We stopped at one of Shivaji's old hill forts, and stepping ashore found our way into the clean-swept little yard of a peasant's home. We sat on a spot where the moonbeams fell glancing off the top of the outer enclosure, and there dined off the eatables we had brought with us. On our way back we let the boat glide down the river. The night brooded over the motionless hills and forests, and on the silent flowing stream of this little *Kalanadi*, throwing over all its moonlight spell. It took us a good long time to reach the mouth of the river, so, instead of returning by sea, we got off the boat there and walked back home over the sands of the beach. It was then far into the night, the sea was without a ripple, even the ever-troubled murmur of the casuarianas was at rest. The shadow of the fringe of trees along the vast expanse of sand hung motionless along its border, and the ring of blue-grey hills around the horizon slept calmly beneath the sky.

Through the deep silence of this illimitable whiteness we few human creatures walked along with our shadows, without a word. When we reached home my sleep had lost itself in something still deeper. The poem which I then wrote is inextricably mingled with that night on the distant seashore. I do not know how it will appeal to the reader apart from the memories with which

Karwar Beach

it is entwined. This doubt led to its being left out of Mohita Babu's edition of my works. I trust that a place given to it among my reminiscences may not be deemed unfitting.

Let me sink down, losing myself in the depths of midnight.
Let the Earth leave her hold of me, let her free me from her obstacle of dust.
Keep your watch from afar, O stars, drunk though you be with moonlight,
And let the horizon hold its wings still around me.
Let there be no song, no word, no sound, no touch; nor sleep, nor awakening,—
But only the moonlight like a swoon of ecstasy over the sky and my being.
The world seems to me like a ship with its countless pilgrims,
Vanishing in the far-away blue of the sky,
Its sailors' song becoming fainter and fainter in the air,
While I sink in the bosom of the endless night, fading away from myself, dwindling into a point.

It is necessary to remark here that merely because something has been written when feelings are brimming over, it is not therefore necessarily good. Such is rather a time when the utterance is thick with emotion. Just as it does not do to have the writer entirely removed from the feeling to which he is giving expression, so also it does not conduce to the truest poetry to have him too close to it. Memory is the brush which can best lay on the true poetic colour. Nearness has too much of the compelling about it and the imagination is not sufficiently free unless it can get away from its influence. Not only in poetry, but in all art, the mind of the artist must attain a certain degree of aloofness—the *creator* within man must be allowed the sole control. If the subject matter gets the better of the creation, the result is a mere replica of the event, not a reflection of it through the Artist's mind.

(37) *Nature's Revenge*

Here in Karwar I wrote the *Prakritir Pratishodha*, Nature's Revenge, a dramatic poem. The hero was a Sanyasi (hermit) who had been striving to gain a victory over Nature by cutting away the bonds of all desires and affections and thus to arrive at a true and profound knowledge of self. A little girl, however, brought him back from his communion with the infinite to the world and into the bondage of human affection. On so coming back the *Sanyasi* realised that the great is to be found in the small, the infinite within the bounds of form, and the eternal freedom of the soul in love. It is only in the light of love that all limits are merged in the limitless.

The sea beach of Karwar is certainly a fit place in which to realise that the beauty of Nature is not a mirage of the imagination, but reflects the joy of the Infinite and thus draws us to lose ourselves in it. Where the universe is expressing itself in the magic of its laws it may not be strange if we miss its infinitude; but where the heart gets into immediate touch with immensity in the beauty of the meanest of things, is any room left for argument?

Nature took the *Sanyasi* to the presence of the Infinite, enthroned on the finite, by the pathway of the heart. In the *Nature's Revenge* there were shown on the one side the wayfarers and the villagers, content with their home-made triviality and unconscious of anything beyond; and on the other the *Sanyasi* busy casting away his all, and himself, into the self-evolved infinite of his imagination. When love bridged the gulf between the two, and the hermit and the householder met, the seeming triviality of the finite and the seeming emptiness of the infinite alike disappeared.

This was to put in a slightly different form the story of my own experience, of the entrancing ray of light which found its way into the depths of the cave into which I had retired away from all touch with the outer world, and made me more fully one with Nature again. This *Nature's Revenge* may be looked upon as an introduction to the whole of my future literary work; or, rather this has been the subject on which all my writings have dwelt—the joy of attaining the Infinite within the finite.

On our way back from Karwar I wrote some songs for the *Nature's Revenge* on board ship. The first one filled me with a great gladness as I sang, and wrote it sitting on the deck:

Mother, leave your darling boy to us,
And let us take him to the field where we graze our cattle.[1]

The sun has risen, the buds have opened, the cowherd boys are going to the pasture; and they would not have the sunlight, the flowers, and their play in the grazing grounds empty. They want their *Shyam* (Krishna) to be with them there, in the midst of all these. They want to see the Infinite in all its carefully adorned loveliness;

[1] This is addressed to Yashoda, mother of Krishna, by his playmates. Yashoda would dress up her darling every morning in his yellow garment with a peacock plume in his hair. But when it came to the point, she was nervous about allowing him, young as he was, to join the other cowherd boys at the pasturage. So it often required a great deal of persuasion before they would be allowed to take charge of him. This is part of the *Vaishnava* parable of the child aspect of Krishna's play with the world. *Tr.*

they have turned out so early because they want to join in its gladsome play, in the midst of these woods and fields and hills and dales—not to admire from a distance, nor in the majesty of power. Their equipment is of the slightest. A simple yellow garment and a garland of wild-flowers are all the ornaments they require. For where joy reigns on every side, to hunt for it arduously, or amidst pomp and circumstances, is to lose it.

Shortly after my return from Karwar, I was married. I was then 22 years of age.

(38) *Pictures and Songs*

Chhabi o Gan, Picture and Songs, was the title of a book of poems most of which were written at this time.

We were then living in a house with a garden in Lower Circular Road. Adjoining it on the south was a large *Busti.*[1] I would often sit near a window and watch the sights of this populous little settlement. I loved to see them at their work and play and rest, and in their multifarious

[1] A Busti is an area thickly packed with shabby tiled huts, with narrow pathways running through, and connecting it with the main street. These are inhabited by domestic servants, the poorer class of artisans and the like. Such settlements were formerly scattered throughout the town even in the best localities, but are now gradually disappearing from the latter. *Tr.*

goings and comings. To me it was all like a living story.

A faculty of many-sightedness possessed me at this time. Each little separate picture I ringed round with the light of my imagination and the joy of my heart; every one of them, moreover, being variously coloured by a pathos of its own. The pleasure of thus separately marking off each picture was much the same as that of painting it, both being the outcome of the desire to see with the mind what the eye sees, and with the eye what the mind imagines.

Had I been a painter with the brush I would doubtless have tried to keep a permanent record of the visions and creations of that period when my mind was so alertly responsive. But that instrument was not available to me. What I had was only words and rhythms, and even with these I had not yet learnt to draw firm strokes, and the colours went beyond their margins. Still, like young folk with their first paint box, I spent the livelong day painting away with the many coloured fancies of my new-born youth. If these pictures are now viewed in the light of that twenty-second year of my life, some features may be discerned even through their crude drawing and blurred colouring.

I have said that the first book of my literary

life came to an end with the *Morning Songs.* The same subject was then continued under a different rendering. Many a page at the outset of this Book, I am sure, is of no value. In the process of making a new beginning much in the way of superfluous preliminary has to be gone through. Had these been leaves of trees they would have duly dropped off. Unfortunately, leaves of books continue to stick fast even when they are no longer wanted. The feature of these poems was the closeness of attention devoted even to trifling things. *Pictures and Songs* seized every opportunity of giving value to these by colouring them with feelings straight from the heart.

Or, rather, that was not it. When the string of the mind is properly attuned to the universe then at each point the universal song can awaken its sympathetic vibrations. It was because of this music roused within that nothing then felt trivial to the writer. Whatever my eyes fell upon found a response within me. Like children who can play with sand or stones or shells or whatever they can get (for the spirit of play is within them), so also we, when filled with the song of youth, become aware that the harp of the universe has its variously tuned strings everywhere stretched, and the nearest may serve as well as any other for our accompaniment, there is no need to seek afar.

(39) *An Intervening Period*

Between the *Pictures and Songs* and the *Sharps and Flats*, a child's magazine called the *Balaka* sprang up and ended its brief days like an annual plant. My second sister-in-law felt the want of an illustrated magazine for children. Her idea was that the young people of the family would contribute to it, but as she felt that that alone would not be enough, she took up the editorship herself and asked me to help with contributions. After one or two numbers of the *Balaka* had come out I happened to go on a visit to Rajnarayan Babu at Deoghur. On the return journey the train was crowded and as there was an unshaded light just over the only berth I could get, I could not sleep. I thought I might as well take this opportunity of thinking out a story for the *Balaka*. In spite of my efforts to get hold of the story it eluded me, but sleep came to the rescue instead. I saw in a dream the stone steps of a temple stained with the blood of victims of the sacrifice;—a little girl standing there with her father asking him in piteous accents: "Father, what is this, why all this blood?" and the father, inwardly moved, trying with a show of gruffness to quiet her questioning. As I awoke I felt I had got my story. I have many more such dream-given stories and other writings as well. This dream episode I worked into the annals of King Gobinda Manikya of Tipperah and made out of it a little serial story, *Rajarshi*, for the *Balaka*.

Those were days of utter freedom from care. Nothing in particular seemed to be anxious to express itself through my life or writings. I had not yet joined the throng of travellers on the path of Life, but was a mere spectator from my roadside window. Many a person hied by on many an errand as I gazed on, and every now and then Spring or Autumn, or the Rains would enter unasked and stay with me for a while.

But I had not only to do with the seasons. There were men of all kinds of curious types who, floating about like boats adrift from their anchorage, occasionally invaded my little room. Some of them sought to further their own ends, at the cost of my inexperience, with many an extraordinary device. But they need not have taken any extraordinary pains to get the better of me. I was then entirely unsophisticated, my own wants were few, and I was not at all clever in distinguishing between good and bad faith. I have often gone on imagining that I was assisting with their school fees students to whom fees were as superfluous as their unread books.

Once a long-haired youth brought me a letter from an imaginary sister in which she asked me to take under my protection this brother of hers who was suffering from the tyranny of a stepmother as imaginary as herself. The brother was not imaginary, that was evident enough. But his sister's letter was as unnecessary for me as expert marksmanship to bring down a bird which cannot fly.

Another young fellow came and informed me that he was studying for the B. A., but could not go up for his examination as he was afflicted with some brain trouble. I felt concerned, but being far from proficient in medical science, or in any other science, I was at a loss what advice to give him. But he went on to explain that he had seen in a dream that my wife had been his mother in a former birth, and that if he could but drink some water which had touched her feet he would get cured. "Perhaps you don't believe in such things," he concluded with a smile. My belief, I said, did not matter, but if he thought he could get cured, he was welcome, with which I procured him a phial of water which was supposed to have touched my wife's feet. He felt immensely better, he said. In the natural course of evolution from water he came to solid food. Then he took up his quarters in a corner of my room and began to hold smoking parties with his friends, till I had to take refuge in flight from the smoke laden air. He gradually proved beyond doubt that his brain might have been diseased, but it certainly was not weak.

After this experience it took no end of proof before I could bring myself to put my trust in children of previous births. My reputation must have spread for I next received a letter from a daughter. Here, however, I gently but firmly drew the line.

All this time my friendship with Babu Srish Chandra Magundar ripened apace. Every evening he and Prija Babu would come to this little room of mine and we would discuss literature and music far into the night. Sometimes a whole day would be spent in the same way. The fact is my *self* had not yet been moulded and nourished into a strong and definite personality and so my life drifted along as light and easy as an autumn cloud.

(40) *Bankim Chandra*

This was the time when my acquaintance with Bankim Babu began. My first sight of him was a matter of long before. The old students of Calcutta University had then started an annual reunion, of which Babu Chandranath Basu was the leading spirit. Perhaps he entertained a hope that at some future time I might acquire the right to be one of them; anyhow I was asked to read a poem on the occasion. Chandranath Babu was then quite a young man. I remember he had translated some martial German poem into English which he proposed to recite himself on the day, and came to rehearse it to us full of enthusiasm. That a warrior poet's ode to his beloved sword should at one time have been his favourite poem will convince the reader that even Chandranath Babu was once young; and moreover that those times were indeed peculiar.

While wandering about in the crush at the Students' reunion, I suddenly came across a figure which at once struck me as distinguished beyond that of all the others and who could not have possibly been lost in any crowd. The features of that tall fair personage shone with such a striking radiance that I could not contain my curiosity about him—he was the only one there whose name I felt concerned to know that day. When I learnt he was Bankim Babu I marvelled all the more, it seemed to me such a wonderful coincidence that his appearance should be as distinguished as his writings. His sharp aquiline nose, his compressed lips, and his keen glance all betokened immense power. With his arms folded across his breast he

two and an effusive appreciation of *Vaishnava* lyrics.

From now I began constantly to meet Bankim Babu. He was then living in Bhabani Dutt's street. I used to visit him frequently, it is true, but there was not much of conversation. I was then of the age to listen, not to talk. I fervently wished we could warm up into some discussion, but my diffidence got the better of my conversational powers. Some days Sanjib Babu [1] would be there reclining on his bolster. The sight would gladden me, for he was a genial soul. He delighted in talking and it was a delight to listen to his talk. Those who have read his prose writing must have noticed how gaily and airily it flows on like the sprightliest of conversation. Very few have this gift of conversation, and fewer still the art of translating it into writing.

This was the time when Pandit Sashadhar rose into prominence. Of him I first heard from Bankim Babu. If I remember right Bankim Babu was also responsible for introducing him to the public. The curious attempt made by Hindu orthodoxy to revive its prestige with the help of western science soon spread all over the country. Theosophy for some time previously had been preparing the ground for such a movement. Not

[1] One of Bankim Babu's brothers.

that Bankim Babu even thoroughly identified himself with this cult. No shadow of Sashadhar was cast on his exposition of Hinduism as it found expression in the *Prachar*—that was impossible.

I was then coming out of the seclusion of my corner as my contributions to these controversies will show. Some of these were satirical verses, some farcical plays, others letters to newspapers. I thus came down into the arena from the regions of sentiment and began to spar in right earnest.

In the heat of the fight I happened to fall foul of Bankim Babu. The history of this remains recorded in the *Prachar* and *Bharati* of those days and need not be repeated here. At the close of this period of antagonism Bankim Babu wrote me a letter which I have unfortunately lost. Had it been here the reader could have seen with what consummate generosity Bankim Babu had taken the sting out of that unfortunate episode.

PART VIII

(41) *The Steamer Hulk*

LURED by an advertisement in some paper my brother Jyotirindra went off one afternoon to an auction sale, and on his return informed us that he had bought a steel hulk for seven thousand rupees; all that now remained being to put in an engine and some cabins for it to become a full-fledged steamer.

My brother must have thought it a great shame that our countrymen should have their tongues and pens going, but not a single line of steamers. As I have narrated before, he had tried to light matches for his country, but no amount of rubbing availed to make them strike. He had also wanted power-looms to work, but after all his travail only one little country towel was born, and then the loom stopped. And now that he wanted Indian steamers to ply, he bought an empty old hulk, which in due course, was filled, not only with engines and cabins, but with loss and ruin as well.

And yet we should remember that all the loss and hardship due to his endeavours fell on him alone, while the gain of experience remained in reserve for the whole country. It is these uncalculating, unbusinesslike spirits who keep the business-fields of the country flooded with their activities. And, though the flood subsides as rapidly as it comes, it leaves behind fertilising silt to enrich the soil. When the time for reaping arrives no one thinks of these pioneers; but those who have cheerfully staked and lost their all, during life, are not likely, after death, to mind this further loss of being forgotten.

On one side was the European Flotilla Company, on the other my brother Jyotirindra alone; and how tremendous waxed that battle of the mercantile fleets, the people of Khulna and Barisal may still remember. Under the stress of competition steamer was added to steamer, loss piled on loss, while the income dwindled till it ceased to be worth while to print tickets. The golden age dawned on the steamer service between Khulna and Barisal. Not only were the passengers carried free of charge, but they were offered light refreshments *gratis* as well! Then was formed a band of volunteers who, with flags and patriotic songs, marched the passengers in procession to the Indian line of steamers. So while there was no want of passengers to carry, every other kind of want began to multiply apace.

Arithmetic remained uninfluenced by patriotic fervour; and while enthusiasm flamed higher and higher to the tune of patriotic songs, three times

My Brother Jyotirindra

three went on steadily making nine on the wrong side of the balance sheet.

One of the misfortunes which always pursues the unbusinesslike is that, while they are as easy to read as an open book, they never learn to read the character of others. And since it takes them the whole of their lifetime and all their resources to find out this weakness of theirs, they never get the chance of profiting by experience. While the passengers were having free refreshments, the staff showed no signs of being starved either, but nevertheless the greatest gain remained with my brother in the ruin he so valiantly faced.

The daily bulletins of victory or disaster which used to arrive from the theatre of action kept us in a fever of excitement. Then one day came the news that the steamer *Swadeshi* had fouled the Howrah bridge and sunk. With this last loss my brother completely overstepped the limits of his resources, and there was nothing for it but to wind up the business.

(42) *Bereavements*

In the meantime death made its appearance in our family. Before this, I had never met Death face to face. When my mother died I was quite a child. She had been ailing for quite a long time, and we did not even know when her malady had taken a fatal turn. She used all along to sleep on a separate bed in the same room with us. Then in the course of her illness she was taken for a boat trip on the river, and on her return a room on the third storey of the inner apartments was set apart for her.

On the night she died we were fast asleep in our room downstairs. At what hour I cannot tell, our old nurse came running in weeping and crying: "O my little ones, you have lost your all!" My sister-in-law rebuked her and led her away, to save us the sudden shock at dead of night. Half awakened by her words, I felt my heart sink within me, but could not make out what had happened. When in the morning we were told of her death, I could not realize all that it meant for me.

As we came out into the verandah we saw my mother laid on a bedstead in the courtyard. There was nothing in her appearance which showed death to be terrible. The aspect which death wore in that morning light was as lovely as a calm and peaceful sleep, and the gulf between life and its absence was not brought home to us.

Only when her body was taken out by the main gateway, and we followed the procession to the cremation ground, did a storm of grief pass through me at the thought that mother would never return by this door and take again her accustomed place in the affairs of her household. The day wore on, we returned from the cremation, and as we turned into our lane I looked up at the house towards my father's rooms on the third storey. He was still in the front verandah sitting motionless in prayer.

She who was the youngest daughter-in-law of the house took charge of the motherless little ones. She herself saw to our food and clothing and all other wants, and kept us constantly near, so that we might not feel our loss too keenly. One of the characteristics of the living is the power to heal the irreparable, to forget the irreplaceable. And in early life this power is strongest, so that no blow penetrates too deeply, no scar is left permanently. Thus the first shadow of death which fell on us left no darkness behind; it departed as softly as it came, only a shadow.

When, in later life, I wandered about like a madcap, at the first coming of spring, with a handful of half-blown jessamines tied in a corner of my muslin scarf, and as I stroked my forehead with the soft, rounded, tapering buds, the touch of my mother's fingers would come back to me; and I clearly realised that the tenderness which dwelt in the tips of those lovely fingers was the very same as that which blossoms every day in the purity of these jessamine buds; and that whether we know it or not, this tenderness is on the earth in boundless measure.

The acquaintance which I made with Death at the age of twenty-four was a permanent one, and its blow has continued to add itself to each succeeding bereavement in an ever lengthening chain of tears. The lightness of infant life can skip aside from the greatest of calamities, but with age evasion is not so easy, and the shock of that day I had to take full on my breast.

That there could be any gap in the unbroken procession of the joys and sorrows of life was a thing I had no idea of. I could therefore see nothing beyond, and this life I had accepted as all in all. When of a sudden death came and in a moment made a gaping rent in its smooth-seeming fabric, I was utterly bewildered. All around, the trees, the soil, the water, the sun, the moon, the stars, remained as immovably true as before; and yet the person who was as truly there, who, through a thousand points of contact with life, mind, and heart, was ever so much more true for me, had vanished in a moment like a dream. What perplexing self-contradiction it all seemed to me as I looked around! How was I ever to reconcile that which remained with that which had gone?

The terrible darkness which was disclosed to me through this rent, continued to attract me night and day as time went on. I would ever and anon return to take my stand there and gaze upon it, wondering what there was left in place of what had gone. Emptiness is a thing man cannot bring himself to believe in; that which is *not*, is untrue; that which is untrue, is not. So our efforts to find something, where we see nothing, are unceasing.

Just as a young plant, surrounded by darkness, stretches itself, as it were on tiptoe, to find its way out into the light, so when death suddenly throws the darkness of negation round the soul it tries and tries to rise into the light of affirmation. And what other sorrow is comparable to the state wherein darkness prevents the finding of a way out of the darkness?

And yet in the midst of this unbearable grief, flashes of joy seemed to sparkle in my mind, now and again, in a way which quite surprised me. That life was not a stable permanent fixture was itself the sorrowful tidings which helped to lighten my mind. That we were not prisoners for ever within a solid stone wall of life was the thought which unconsciously kept coming uppermost in rushes of gladness. That which I had held I was made to let go—this was the sense of loss which distressed me,—but when at the same moment I

(43) *The Rains and Autumn*

According to the Hindu calendar, each year is ruled by a particular planet. So have I found that in each period of life a particular season assumes a special importance. When I look back to my childhood I can best recall the rainy days. The wind-driven rain has flooded the verandah floor. The row of doors leading into the rooms are all closed. Peari, the old scullery maid, is coming from the market, her basket laden with vegetables, wading through the slush and drenched with the rain. And for no rhyme or reason I am careering about the verandah in an ecstasy of joy.

This also comes back to me:—I am at school, our class is held in a colonnade with mats as outer screens; cloud upon cloud has come up during the afternoon, and they are now heaped up, covering the sky; and as we look on, the rain comes down in close thick showers, the thunder at intervals rumbling long and loud; some mad woman with nails of lightning seems to be rending the sky from end to end; the mat walls tremble under the blasts of wind as if they would be blown in; we can hardly see to read, for the darkness. The Pandit gives us leave to close our books. Then leaving the storm to do the romping and roaring for us, we keep swinging our dangling legs; and my mind goes right away across the far-off unending moor through which the Prince of the fairy tale passes.

I remember, moreover, the depth of the *Sravan* [1] nights. The pattering of the rain finding its way through the gaps of my slumber, creates within a gladsome restfulness deeper than the deepest sleep. And in the wakeful intervals I pray that the morning may see the rain continue, our lane under water, and the bathing platform of the tank submerged to the last step.

But at the age of which I have just been telling, Autumn is on the throne beyond all doubt. Its life is to be seen spread under the clear transparent leisure of *Aswin*.[2] And in the molten gold of this autumn sunshine, softly reflected from the fresh dewy green outside, I am pacing the verandah and composing, in the mode *Jogiya*, the song:

In this morning light I do not know what it is that my heart desires.

The autumn day wears on, the house gong sounds 12 noon, the mode changes; though my

[1] The month corresponding to July–August, the height of the rainy season.

[2] The month of Aswin corresponds to September–October, the long vacation time for Bengal.

mind is still filled with music, leaving no room for call of work or duty; and I sing:

What idle play is this with yourself, my heart, through the listless hours?

Then in the afternoon I am lying on the white floorcloth of my little room, with a drawing book trying to draw pictures,—by no means an arduous pursuit of the pictorial muse, but just a toying with the desire to make pictures. The most important part is that which remains in the mind, and of which not a line gets drawn on the paper. And in the meantime the serene autumn afternoon is filtering through the walls of this little Calcutta room filling it, as a cup, with golden intoxication.

I know not why, but all my days of that period I see as if through this autumn sky, this autumn light—the autumn which ripened for me my songs as it ripens the corn for the tillers; the autumn which filled my granary of leisure with radiance; the autumn which flooded my unburdened mind with an unreasoning joy in fashioning song and story.

The great difference which I see between the Rainy-season of my childhood and the Autumn of my youth is that in the former it is outer Nature which closely hemmed me in keeping me entertained with its numerous troupe, its variegated make-up, its medley of music; while the festivity which goes on in the shining light of autumn is in man himself. The play of cloud and sunshine is left in the background, while the murmurs of joy and sorrow occupy the mind. It is our gaze which gives to the blue of the autumn sky its wistful tinge and human yearning which gives poignancy to the breath of its breezes.

My poems have now come to the doors of men. Here informal goings and comings are not allowed. There is door after door, chamber within chamber. How many times have we to return with only a glimpse of the light in the window, only the sound of the pipes from within the palace gates lingering in our ears. Mind has to treat with mind, will to come to terms with will, through many tortuous obstructions, before giving and taking can come about. The foundation of life, as it dashes into these obstacles, splashes and foams over in laughter and tears, and dances and whirls through eddies from which one cannot get a definite idea of its course.

(44) *Sharps and Flats*

Sharps and Flats is a serenade from the streets in front of the dwelling of man, a plea to be allowed an entry and a place within that house of mystery.

> This world is sweet,—I do not want to die.
> I wish to dwell in the ever-living life of Man.

This is the prayer of the individual to the universal life.

When I started for my second voyage to England, I made the acquaintance on board ship of Asutosh Chaudhuri. He had just taken the M. A. degree of the Calcutta University and was on his way to England to join the Bar. We were together only during the few days the steamer took from Calcutta to Madras, but it became quite evident that depth of friendship does not depend upon length of acquaintance. Within this short time he so drew me to him by his simple natural qualities of heart, that the previous life-long gap in our acquaintance seemed always to have been filled with our friendship.

When Ashu came back from England he became one of us.[1] He had not as yet had time or opportunity to pierce through all the barriers with which his profession is hedged in, and so become completely immersed in it. The money-bags of his clients had not yet sufficiently loosened the strings which held their gold, and Ashu was still an enthusiast in gathering honey from various gardens of literature. The spirit of literature which then saturated his being had nothing of the mustiness of library morocco about it, but was fragrant with the scent of unknown exotics from over the

[1] Referring to his marriage with the writer's niece, Pratibha. *Tr.*

seas. At his invitation I enjoyed many a picnic amidst the spring time of those distant woodlands.

He had a special taste for the flavour of French literature. I was then writing the poems which came to be published in the volume entitled *Kadi o Komal*, Sharps and Flats. Ashu could discern resemblances between many of my poems and old French poems he knew. According to him the common element in all these poems was the attraction which the play of world-life had for the poet, and this had found varied expression in each and every one of them. The unfulfilled desire to enter into this larger life was the fundamental motive throughout.

"I will arrange and publish these poems for you," said Ashu, and accordingly that task was entrusted to him. The poem beginning *This world is sweet* was the one he considered to be the key-note of the whole series and so he placed it at the beginning of the volume.

Ashu was very possibly right. When in childhood I was confined to the house, I offered my heart in my wistful gaze to outside nature in all its variety through the openings in the parapet of our inner roof-terrace. In my youth the world of men in the same way exerted a powerful attraction on me. To that also I was then an outsider and looked out upon it from the roadside.

My mind standing on the brink called out, as it were, with an eager waving of hands to the ferry-man sailing away across the waves to the other side. For Life longed to start on life's journey.

It is not true that my peculiarly isolated social condition was the bar to my plunging into the midst of the world-life. I see no sign that those of my countrymen who have been all their lives in the thick of society feel, any more than I did, the touch of its living intimacy. The life of our country has its high banks, and its flight of steps, and, on its dark waters falls the cool shade of the ancient trees, while from within the leafy branches over-head the *koel* cooes forth its ravishing old-time song. But for all that it is stagnant water. Where is its current, where are the waves, when does the high tide rush in from the sea?

Did I then get from the neighbourhood on the other side of our lane an echo of the victorious pæan with which the river, falling and rising, wave after wave, cuts its way through walls of stone to the sea? No! My life in its solitude was simply fretting for want of an invitation to the place where the festival of world-life was being held.

Man is overcome by a profound depression while nodding through his voluptuously lazy hours of seclusion, because in this way he is deprived of full commerce with life. Such is the despondency from which I have always painfully struggled to get free. My mind refused to respond to the cheap intoxication of the political movements of those days, devoid, as they seemed, of all strength of national consciousness, with their complete ignorance of the country, their supreme indifference to real service of the motherland. I was tormented by a furious impatience, an intolerable dissatisfaction with myself and all around me. Much rather, I said to myself, would I be an Arab Bedouin!

While in other parts of the world there is no end to the movement and clamour of the revelry of free life, we, like the beggar maid, stand outside and longingly look on. When have we had the wherewithal to deck ourselves for the occasion and go and join in it? Only in a country where the spirit of separation reigns supreme, and innumerable petty barriers divide one from another, need this longing to realise the larger life of the world in one's own remain unsatisfied.

I strained with the same yearning towards the world of men in my youth, as I did in my childhood towards outside nature from within the chalk-ring drawn round me by the servants. How rare, how unattainable, how far away it seemed! And yet if we cannot get into touch with it, if from it no breeze can blow, no current come, if no road be there for the free goings and comings of travellers, then the dead things that accumulate around us never get removed, but continue to be heaped up till they smother all life.

During the Rains there are only dark clouds and showers. And in the Autumn there is the play of light and shade in the sky, but that is not all-absorbing; for there is also the promise of corn in the fields. So in my poetical career, when the rainy season was in the ascendant there were only my vaporous fancies which stormed and showered; my utterance was misty, my verses were wild. And with the *Sharps and Flats* of my Autumn, not only was there the play of cloud-effects in the sky, but out of the ground crops were to be seen rising. Then, in the commerce with the world of reality, both language and metre attempted definiteness and variety of form.

Thus ends another Book. The days of coming together of inside and outside, kin and stranger, are closing in upon my life. My life's journey has now to be completed through the dwelling places of men. And the good and evil, joy and sorrow, which it thus encountered, are not to be lightly viewed as pictures. What makings and breakings, victories and defeats, clashings and minglings, are here going on!

I have not the power to disclose and display the

supreme art with which the Guide of my life is joyfully leading me through all its obstacles, antagonisms and crookednesses towards the fulfilment of its innermost meaning. And if I cannot make clear all the mystery of this design, whatever else I may try to show is sure to prove misleading at every step. To analyse the image is only to get at its dust, not at the joy of the artist.

So having escorted them to the door of the inner sanctuary I take leave of my readers.

Printed in the United States of America